UNDER ATTACK BUT EQUIPPED TO STAND

BISHOP CLIFTON JONES

PRESS

DEDICATION

This book is dedicated to the entire body of Christ with sincere prayer that you will discover exactly how tough you are in Christ and how well equipped you are to stand.

THE TABLE OF CONTENTS:

The Difference An Understanding Makes 15

The Real Trouble-Make 27

Good Men Do Suffer Bad Things 41

Trouble Is A Good Time To Know The Lord........59

Encouraging Words In A Storm 91

If You Are Sold Out, You Can Hold Out..............107

You Will Never Walk Alone.................................121

Anticipated Trouble 139

PREFACE

I do not know of any other writer that has congruously written to the saints in such a purposeful way as has Bishop Clifton Jones. He seems to have divine insight into the crucial needs of the people of God for this day and time. And if the saints are in need of anything today, it's the concern and insight shown by Bishop Jones in his encouraging, yet indicting writing.

One can readily see from his previous books that Bishop Jones is not trying to make the saints feel badly about their failures. On the contrary, while his writing deals very sharply with our failures, they do so in an atmosphere of nurture. Bishop Jones has a passion for helping the saints.

Anyone that doubts Bishop's devotion to the well-being of the saints need do no more than read this book. In fact, a cursory look at the chapter headings will reveal the warmth of an empathetic father who understands both the nuance of life and the inexplicable power of the God whom we serve.

May God open your heart as you receive the message inspired by God and passed on by Bishop Clifton Jones

Jesse Battle

St. Louis, Mo.

INTRODUCTION:

It has been my observation that a large percentage of Christians find themselves inadequate when it comes to being prepared for life's difficulties. The majority seems to think that nothing but good should come their way after entering into the services of the Lord God of heaven; however, just the opposite is true. Once we get involved in the army of the Lord, we are sure to provoke the anger of God's arch enemy the devil, and he is sure to do everything within his power to cause our defeat; however the Lord has made provisions for our strong deliverance and our ultimate victory.

We should not be taken by surprise when the enemy attacks. He is just being and doing what he is doomed to do. His anger is being expressed toward the followers of the Lord Jesus because he knows that he is no match for our Lord himself; therefore, he has to settle for someone that he feels will cower in the face of his threats and bluffs.

I am fascinated when I consider the measure of confidence the Lord has in His ability and the enabling power He has invested in His believing children. He fills us with Himself and leaves us in these same old corrupt bodies while yet living in this wicked world, and He expects us to be more than conquers. It's good just to be a conquerors, but He has made us more than conquerors through Him that loves us. Selah! Praise God!

As long as we abide in Him, there is nothing anyone, nor anything can do to bring about our defeat. He is <u>truly</u> "our refuge and strength." What the Lord is to us and in us stands out even the more when we are under attack and the sooner we understand this fact, the sooner we send the enemy on his way.

The Apostle Paul seemed to have grown up in Christ to appreciate trouble. We learn from him that trouble is short-lived and spiritually rewarding. The more we believe this fact, the less damage the enemy would do to us. When we line our conversation and behavior up with that of the Apostle Paul, we know that trouble is fast-forwarding our faith level to a place where trouble pays off in our lives. Trouble works for our good. Every time the adversary intends it for evil, God turns it into good.

This man of God encountered trouble from day one. He was often imprisoned, beaten, stoned, ship-wrecked, cold and naked, hungry and was often accused by false brothers, but to according to his elec-trifying testimony, none of those things moved him. After making an appeal to the Lord for a way out of his difficulties, the Lord gave him a word of encouragement; he was then ready to move on in his life.

"And he said unto me, My grace is sufficient for thee: for my strength is made perfect in weakness. Most gladly therefore will I rather glory in my infirmities, that the power of Christ may rest upon me.

10 Therefore I take pleasure in infirmities, in reproaches, in necessities, in persecutions, in distresses for Christ's sake: for when I am weak, then am I strong." 2 Cor 12:9 KJV

When we prepare for the worst, we are sure to have what it takes to deal with whatever life brings our way, but if we are looking for a life of ease, it will not be found in the Christian walk.

We need not fear and neither do we have need of seeking out the enemy. He will do the seeking. He wants to find someone that he can tear apart—to make an example of that wounded soul. We are told by the Word of God to stand fast when he attacks. The Word of God is our foundation and our weapon. As long as we stay with the principle of the Scriptures, we are sure to cause the devil to flee.

We need to engrave this truth in our spirit, and "hold it to be self evident" that whatsoever the enemy is allowed to do to us is sure to make improvements in the lives of those that believe God.

"After you have suffered a little while, our God, who is full of kindness through Christ, will give you his eternal glory. He personally will come and pick you up, and set you firmly in place, and make you stronger than ever." 1 Peter 5:10 TLB

Since we know from the Word of God that everything works for the good of those who love the Lord, our main focus should be on loving the Lord and letting Him help us to deal with everything else. We should not fear being attacked; we should fear not loving the Lord with our whole heart, soul, mind and spirit.

THE DIFFERENCE AN UNDERSTANDING MAKES

One of the arresting points about the Christian life is the fact that the majority of us enter into it totally ignorant of what to expect. No doubt, none of us could fathom the measure of opposition that an attempt at righteous living invites upon us. However, Jesus plainly taught those who followed Him to expect and accept trouble as a necessary part of righteous living.

> *"Blessed are they which are persecuted for righteousness' sake: for theirs is the kingdom of heaven.*
>
> *11 Blessed are ye, when men shall revile you, and persecute you, and shall say all manner of evil against you falsely, for my sake.*
>
> *12 Rejoice, and be exceeding glad: for great is your reward in heaven: for so persecuted*

they the prophets which were before you."-
Matt 5:10-12

According to the teachings of Jesus, it is not necessary to go out looking for trouble; all one has to do is walk close to Him and trouble will come. Jesus also gave words to help adjust our attitudes so that when trouble calls, we would not take it personally; neither would we think that the unexpected had happened.

The teaching of the righteous being persecuted is supported by both Testaments. Many bore the description of Christ in the Old Testament. One of the persons who fit that type was Joseph. Jacob, on his dying bed, enlarged upon the treatment that Joseph had received. Those of us who have read the story know how he was treated and why he was treated that way.

"Joseph is a fruitful bough, even a fruitful bough by a well; whose branches run over the wall:

23 The archers have sorely grieved him, and shot at him, and hated him:

24 But his bow abode in strength, and the arms of his hands were made strong by the hands of the mighty God of Jacob; (from thence is the shepherd, the stone of Israel :)"- Gen 49:22 -24

You may note that Joseph was not only severely treated, but he was at the same time equipped to stand. His standing was the hope of the future of Israel; in other words, Joseph saved his entire family nation from certain death.

Since we know we are dealing with a matter that is here to stay, we would be better off to acquaint ourselves with standing.

Let us clarify our application of two words in our title:

These two words highlight two realities in our subject and neither is any less real than the other. One informs us that we are exposed to the attack of someone who wants to hurt or destroy us. However, the latter tells us that we have been "furnished with the needed resources," and we don't have to be defeated, for we are equipped to STAND.

I choose to believe in the existence of both, but my focus is more on the latter since I have no say so about when I am to be attacked or by what means I will be attacked. I just pray God that He will continue to enable me to acquaint myself with the equipment that supports my unrelinquishing STAND. Although we do not know when or how we are going to be attacked, we know that we are. Therefore, we must build ourselves up on the fact that God has equipped us to weather the storms that come. I can speak from experience as well as from observation. When we grow stronger, we are more grateful for having been attacked and enlarged by knowing that our equipment works. However, if the troubling experience finds us in the wrong attitude, and we fail the test, the results is anger, wherein we accuse God of leaving us, and we go about sulking and pouting, and miss out on our promotion to the next grade.

The latter is what the enemy would like to see us do. It delights him when we feel so self-important that we feel we are above life's problems. And you and I know that nothing is further from the truth. Now. This is a fact we must keep clear in our minds; no one, including Jesus Himself, could live so holy or so good that trouble is removed from his/her paths of life. Only the Devil himself would like to plant such a deceitful seed. He knows that if he can get us to buy into that deception, he can more easily destroy us when we enter into our hour of persecution.

Our attitudes toward persecution play a very important role in how well we handle our difficulties. If we feel that we are suffering unduly (something we do not deserve), we will surely be hung out to dry, so to speak. We must keep in mind that it is our own lifestyle we have chosen that is inviting difficulties into our lives.

When we look at how well the Lord has equipped us, it should make us bold in the face of opposition because we know that His equipment is well able to deliver us from the hand of the enemy. The consolation in our tribulations is the blessed assurance that He is ever near and He is well able to keep us from falling.

I am willing to go so far as to say that over half of the battle is in our mentality; the battle is won or lost in the way we perceive what is happening. Satan recognizes this fact; that is why he is so skillful at mind games. He will use anything he can to bombard the mind: worry, fear, pain, sorrow, disappointment, heart ache, depression; you name it and he will try it.

Keep in mind; if you ever feel that you are at the bottom, you can be sure that your next move is up. If you are already at the bottom, you cannot go any lower. *You just need to talk to* yourself, (and don't worry about anybody wondering about your sanity). You should rather that we think that you are a bit off when you are not, than for us to think you are on when, in fact, you are off. Therefore, talk to yourself; let your ears hear your mouth say positive faith building-things that would help raise your position and strengthen your stand. Speaking God's truth concerning you is a part of your equipment.

Get it in you mind that this is a good fight and you are in it for the duration. If trouble is a part of the plan, bring it on because you must successfully pass your course because you want your crown. Furthermore, anything that is worth having, is worth fighting for with everything you have within you, so roll up your spiritual sleeves and gives the enemy one of the best fights he has ever known. Remember the enemy knows when you know that you are more than a conqueror. He can tell when you are serious about your journey, since he has gathered enough information on you to know that you won't surrender without a fight. We are given too many good examples of triumph over tragedy for us to allow the enemy to talk us out of the fight.

It is a fact that "winners never quit and quitters never win." This was told to me by a high school coach. I have held on to these words since the day they first admonished me because they make so much battlefield sense to me. He used them to inspire us to play better ball. I want to tell you that they work in making my life more meaningful because those words inspired me to keep on trying even when all hope seemed lost.

The trail of examples runs from Genesis to Revelation, and Jesus Himself climaxed it with His own life-saving sacrifice on the Cross. He could have quit, but winning was set before Him. He would not let suffering prevent Him from achieving His heavenly appointed mission. We are encouraged by the Word of God to follow His example along with the examples that were left by those that believed in the Lord Jesus Christ as Lord and Savior and won.

"Wherefore seeing we also are compassed about with so great a cloud of witnesses, let us lay aside every weight, and the sin which doth so easily beset us, and let us run with patience the race that is set before us,

2 Looking unto Jesus the author and finisher of our faith; who for the joy that was set before him endured the cross, despising the shame, and is set down at the right hand of the throne of God.

3 For consider him that endured such contradiction of sinners against himself, lest ye be wearied and faint in your minds."
- Heb 12:1-3

Examples serve as stimuli to motivate us to try even harder and never give up. When it comes to living right, we have to be truly motivated by the Spirit of God not to give in to the pressures of this life. We should thank the Lord that He has truly equipped us to take the heat that this life generates. There is yet another thing we need to understand. That is, the enemy is not just after us because we are so successful. He hates the one that we love and will do anything within his power to hurt the heart of God. The best way for him to achieve this ominous goal, is to get us confused, depressed, discouraged, disappointed and heart broken to the degree that we walk away from the Lord. Once we are turned away from our Lord, our source of help and strength and power, we have no place else to turn. Where can we go? He has the words of eternal life, abundant life — real life!! We are left vulnerable to the enemy's attacks without protection. This is why he tries so intensely to get us to think of trouble as a earns of destruction and an attack from God for our shortcomings. He wants our minds so cloudy to God's purpose that we cannot see the real truth and rest upon the promise that the Lord is with us regardless of the circumstances.

Satan challenges us every step of the way as we even attempt to study and emulate the examples left us in the Word of God. One of his attack weapons is to infiltrate minds with the thought that what God did back then is no longer His way of operation. He wants us to believe that the quality of faith that the Bible characters possessed was superior to the faith God allows us today. That is just another one of his desperate lies that he offers to disturb our minds to keep us from being fully persuaded.

The Apostle Paul said it best when he wrote to the Roman Christians concerning the purpose of what was written:

"Christ didn't please himself. As the Psalmist said, "He came for the very purpose of suffering under the insults of those who were against the Lord." 4 These things that were written in the Scriptures so long ago are to teach us patience and to encourage us so that we will look forward expectantly to the time when God will conquer sin and death.

5 May God who gives patience, steadiness, and encouragement help you to live in complete harmony with each other-each with the attitude of Christ toward the other."
- Rom 15:3-5 TLB

I am persuaded that the Lord wants us to draw from the examples of those that have gone before us and to be encouraged that He will never leave us to do battle alone. He is forever with us; therefore, all we need to do is to recognize it, claim it and stand on it.

"Wherefore take unto you the whole armour of God, that ye may be able to withstand in the evil day, and having done all, to stand.

14 Stand therefore, having your loins girt about with truth, and having on the breastplate of righteousness;"- Eph 6:13-14

God can never be found guilty of leaving His children unprotected. He might be accused of doing so but there is no evidence to support such falsehood. Having the presence of the Lord with us places the majority on our side. Whenever we are in doubt of His protection speak up, remind yourself that the Lord is with us, and the Lord's presence, all we only need do is ask Him for revelation and for the opening of our spiritual eyes. When we see things through the eyes of the Spirit, we are sure to take heart to stand.

Our reaping a good harvest depends on our standing; if we continue to stand we are sure to "come again rejoicing bringing in the sheaves". We must keep on doing all the good we can until the Lord brings to pass His will in our lives.

"And let us not be weary in well doing: for in due season we shall reap, if we faint not."
- Gal 6:9

The equipment of Patience plays a major role in our battles with the attacker. The more patient we are the better our chances of outlasting our troubles. If we allow our troubles to outlast us, then we suffer defeat. However, when we outlast our troubles, we receive the credit, and we are blessed to continue. Patience helps us to overcome Satan's fear tactics. He has always been known for his use of fear. He uses fear to offset faith. This is why it is not good to draw your conclusions from just what you see because fear will blind the eyes causing you to see more trouble than there is. We need only to pray a prayer similar to the one that was prayed by Elisha when his servant was having difficulty comprehending what he was saying about the majority being on their side.

"And when the servant of the man of God was risen early, and gone forth, behold, an host compassed the city both with horses and chariots. And his servant said unto him, Alas, my master! How shall we do?

16 And he answered, Fear not: for they that be with us are more than they that be with them.

17 And Elisha prayed, and said, LORD, I pray thee, open his eyes, that he may see. And the LORD opened the eyes of the young man; and he saw: and, behold, the mountain was full of horses and chariots of fire round about Elisha."- 2 Kings 6:15-17

One takes on a new boldness once the realization kicks in that he or she is backed by the majority. When the young man *saw* the supporting cast that they had with them, he was no longer afraid. He could *see* that the Lord had not left them alone and neither were they out numbered. **"Blessed are they that have not seen and yet have believed".** We may not see bands of angels surrounding us for protection but we do have the Word of God giving us all we need to stand on.

I believe that the Word of God provides us with the many examples of what God has done so that we take courage and believe that what He did for others, He will also do for us. After all, we are His children, and any responsible parents are expected to protect their own children. The Lord wants us to learn how to lean and depend on Him. Learning this principle we find that no weapon formed against us shall prosper; and that we will emerge from every battle more than conquerors.

"Then upon Jahaziel the son of Zechariah, the son of Benaiah, the son of Jeiel, the son of Mattaniah, a Levite of the sons of Asaph, came the Spirit of the LORD in the midst of the congregation;

15 And he said, Hearken ye, all Judah, and ye inhabitants of Jerusalem, and thou king Jehoshaphat, Thus saith the LORD unto you, Be not afraid nor dismayed by reason of this great multitude; for the battle is not yours, but God's.

16 To morrow go ye down against them: behold, they come up by the cliff of Ziz; and ye shall find them at the end of the brook, before the wilderness of Jeruel.

17 Ye shall not need to fight in this battle: set yourselves, stand ye still, and see the salvation of the LORD with you, O Judah and Jerusalem: fear not, nor be dismayed; to morrow go out against them: for the LORD will be with you."- 2 Chron 20:14-17

These consoling words were spoken when the picture was extremely dark and all hope seemed loss, but God sent His Word to let His servant know that it was His battle. When it is God's battle, we just need to learn how to step back and let God handle it His way. The Lord fights the battle and credits us with the benefits. However, when the Lord fights the battle, He does expect us to worship and give Him thanks.

"Ye are of God, little children, and have overcome them: because greater is he that is in you, than he that is in the world."
- 1 John 4:4

We have an inner protection that only needs recognizing, when we learn to lean and depend on Jesus, our equipment is activated, and there is no match for us in the entire universe because the greater one lives in us.

THE REAL TROUBLE-MAKER

In the light of all I've said, for sure there is a real troublemaker who prowls around seeking the destruction of as many as he can destroy. The number one candidates on his hit list are believers who proclaim God's power and promises. Nothing pleases him more than to shut our mouths. How he does it doesn't matter to him at all just as long as he can get the job done.

> *"Be careful-watch out for attacks from Satan, your great enemy. He prowls around like a hungry, roaring lion, looking for some victim to tear apart. 9 Stand firm when he attacks. Trust the Lord; and remember that other Christians all around the world are going through these sufferings too." 1 Peter 5:8-9 (TLB)*

Another fact concerning this matter is that Satan's hatred toward us is due to his animosity towards our Lord. The only way he can get back at our Lord is to try to destroy those whom God loves; and that's you and me. His jealousy towards us is based upon the fact that we have embraced the God that has divorced Satan without hope of reconciliation. We love Him whom Satan hates. Satan detests the idea that you and I will live in his world but not live like his citizens. He is stirred and greatly disturbed by the fact that we are going to be walking on his turf while claiming citizenship in the place that he left. So He has decreed that if anybody makes it through here, they must have a made-up mind. Only the strong shall survive; better yet, only those who trust and obey can stand. It is not our battle; the battle is the Lord's!

Although the Lord never promised us a trouble free relationship, He did promise to never leave us. This promise is the Christian's hope and a fresh reminder that the greater one lives in us.

No one knows better than Satan that he is already defeated; however, he heartedly refuses to act as though he has been conquered. Satan uses every known method available to him to encourage faith in his wicked ability.

Ignorance of the Word of God is one of Satan's strongest weapons. Nothing else has contributed to the overthrow of Christians more than ignorance. It is little wonder that Satan loves to distract us from studying the Word of God, and assembling ourselves where the Word is being ministered. He knows that if he can keep us ignorant, he can control us or get us to do things against the will of God.

> *"My people are destroyed for lack of knowledge: because thou hast rejected knowledge, I will also reject thee, that thou shalt be no priest to me: seeing thou hast forgotten the law of thy God, I will also forget thy children."- Hos 4:6*

The better we equip ourselves with the Word of God, the better better our defense. We know that sin is one of Satan's products which, he feels, will bring every man down. It is a fact that Christians do sometimes sin. However, a real child of God will not return to sinning as a pattern. In other words, we are out of the sinning business because we have found a better way that leads to life-and we would rather live than die.

One of the reasons Satan pushes sin so freely is because he feels that no one can indulge in sin without getting hooked. But for the grace of God, this is one time he would be right; however, those of us that have tasted of the Bread of Life (Jesus) know that there is none like Him for conquering sin. Those of us who find delight in our relationship with the Lord can be sure that the enemy will take notice of us and try to bring sin between us and our Master.

Ever since the enemy lost his relationship with the Lord, he has firmly set out to prevent everyone else from having a supernatural relationship with God. When we look at the book of Job, we see that

Job's troubles were not as some supposed. They were permitted by Him but they were brought by Satan. God did not make trouble for Job; neither was He afraid of Job failing or becoming a failure. God knew what He had put in Job. He knew that His equipment would stand under Satan's testing. Satan was the one who was experimenting and accusing. He showed us that he doesn't know everything. If he did, he would have known that Job would not crack under pressure. He makes it his business to watch what's going on so that he will know how to scheme. It was his watchfulness that brought Job into consideration. Job was a threat to all he thought to accomplish. Job was rich, but his heart was not set on his riches. Job had a large, well balanced family and Satan is known to be a family destroyer. Job had the wealth to bless others. Above all, he was in love with God; Satan is totally against all of the above.

Satan is not against us being rich, that is, if he can get us to focus our attention on what we have to the neglect of Him who allowed us to have it. In other words, if we allow our blessings to overshadow the one who blesses, Satan is happy. But if we bless the one who blesses for the blessings, we anger Satan to no end.

"Now there was a day when the sons of God came to present themselves before the LORD, and Satan came also among them.
7 And the LORD said unto Satan, Whence comest thou? Then Satan answered the

LORD, and said, From going to and fro in the earth, and from walking up and down in it.

8 And the LORD said unto Satan, Hast thou considered my servant Job, that there is none like him in the earth, a perfect and an upright man, one that feareth God, and escheweth evil?

9 Then Satan answered the LORD, and said, Doth Job fear God for nought?"- Job 1:6-9 When God questioned Satan about his excursion, Satan made it known hat he was looking for someone to devour. The Lord asked him if he had considered His servant Job. The Lord didn't just leave it at that; He gave some accolades that stirred Satan the more to want a piece of Job. After hearing what the Lord said, Satan started into his role as accuser, Satan knew all along that Job was on his hit list, but he wanted it to sound like God had put Job on the untouchable list. Satan made it sound like Job had modern day mentally; that is to say, he was doing what he was doing because he was being so well paid.
"Why shouldn't he when you pay him so well?" Satan scoffed."- Job 1:9 TLB

Satan's mind-set is that God has to keep doing something tangible for His servants in order for them to love Him. Satan thought like that then and he thinks like that now. But I say he was lying then and he is a liar now. I am persuaded that there are some people who love Jesus aside from what He has blessed them with They know how to enjoy the blessings without forgetting the one who blesses.

Because of Satan's philosophy concerning God's blessings, he seeks to plant that seed in the minds of men. He would have men to believe that blessings are synonymous to a trouble free life. When trouble strikes in the life of a believer, Satan is quick to point out that the believer doesn't deserve this kind of treatment from anybody. By pointing out our difficulties, Satan hopes we will lose our balance and charge God with reckless regards. He would like to see us abandon the meeting place like Adam did after he ate the forbidden fruit. His deep desire is to put a breach between God and man. He knows that when man falls out with God, man is susceptible to his influence.

Satan had hoped to accomplish this purpose when he got permission to attack Job's family and possessions. He wanted Job's family because he hates happy families. As long as families are warring among themselves, Satan is happy; but when there is love and harmony, he is busy plotting how to destroy their happiness. He hates happy people because they serve as a reminder of what he once had, and what he will never know again. He is daily busy trying to spread sadness, if he can make one sad, that helps him sell his lies of how-to-be happy. Many souls are going into eternity deceived, thinking that Satan and this world have more to make one happy than the

Lord has. That is a lie from the pits of hell your worst day with Jesus is better than you best day following the lies of the devil.

Another reason it bothers the enemy to see people happy, is he knows if they continue with the Lord, they will end up where he used to be, and that thought torments him to no end.

I believe the best way we can strike back at the enemy is by being happy, let him shoot his best shot and we continue to bless the Lord with all of our heart, mind and strength. When we do that we send a message to hell, that out of all we've been through we still have joy. Just having Jesus is enough to rejoice in and the fact that He intends to take us home with Him is a tremendous blessing!

Job showed real commitment to the spiritual welfare of his children by offering sacrifice just in the event they had stepped over the line and sinned against God.

> *"When these birthday parties ended-and sometimes they lasted several days-Job would summon his children to him and sanctify them, getting up early in the morning and offering a burnt offering for each of them. For Job said, "Perhaps my sons have sinned and turned away from God in their hearts." This was Job's regular practice."*
> *- Job 1:5 TLB*

Job had real concern for the welfare of the souls of his children. This too will anger Satan because he wants us to feel far removed from the spiritual state of our families. When we love God and love our families, we are demonstrating what Jesus came for; He came to set the captives free. Love for the brotherhood starts at home.

"And so I am giving a new commandment to you now-love each other just as much as I love you. 35 Your strong love for each other will prove to the world that you are my disciples." John 13:34-35 TLB

It would delight Satan to no end to destroy every family that has connections to the Lord Jesus Christ. To do so would give support to his claim that no family or person on the face of this earth can enjoy a life of happiness. To make his lie appear true, he seeks to fill lives with misery, pain, heartache, tragedy, hardship, sickness and all forms of disaster. He wants men to curse God for the day they were born, and blame him as being a respecter of person.

However, God's commitment to us through Job is clear, that one does not have to lose his mind just because he has lost his or her earthly possessions, this includes offsprings. If Satan had known that Job would not crack under pressure, He would have tried something different on Job. Job is a good example for anyone that suffers the loss of children, possessions or even pain in the body. Job is saying today, you can lose earthly connections and yet maintain heavenly contact. Earthly possessions and family ties are not interwoven with the Spirit of God. In other words, to lose one does not necessarily say that you would lose the other.

I would really hate to think that I had anything that I could lose and especially, my losing any earthly possession would lead to my forsaking the Lord. However, if I do, I sure hope the Lord would reveal it to me real soon so that I can replace it with a deeper love for Him.

I am sure that after Satan killed Job's children, and Job didn't crack, Satan knew he had picked the wrong person for his object lesson. You see, he loves to pick those who start whining and wincing at the first sign of trouble; those who will faint at the first sign of heat; those who talk down when they are up and scared when they are secure.

There is no proof of Job having a different reaction toward the loss of his children from his reaction toward the loss of his substances. We can be technical and say he didn't fall down and worship until he heard about his children; however, the messenger that told him about his substance had just finished speaking when word came about his children. No matter how we choose to view it, there is one thing that is certain; Job was able to continue doing what he had been known to do before this all happen. And that is, he was able to worship the true and living God.

It would do you and me well to ask ourselves the question, "Would God continues to be God with us if we suffered such great loss? Or would we be so devastated that we would have no Spirit left to worship?" We may not be able to answer this question today, but we sure do need to have it settled in our hearts what we feel would be best or what we think we would do in a similar situation because "As a man thinketh in his heart so is he."

Now that we see what Job did and can somewhat see what is on Satan's mind, it would be to our advantage to prepare accordingly. We can see that Satan would like to break up our relationship and fellowship with the Lord, and he could care less about how he does it or who he uses to help get the job done. Satan just wants to see us and God at odds.

I pray that the next time you are under a severe attack; you would not give undue attention to the thing or things that are happening, but that you will remember what the enemy is trying to do. Satan would like to make our lives so unpleasant that God would be far removed from our minds. Satan sends out his hit men (little flunky demons) with an assignment to make us so miserable that we would do anything for relief or a quick fix. When we resist his wicked and evil plots, he will place us on his special hit list. Once we make Satan's hit list, we can be sure that his mafia or hit men are going to stalk us—seek to devour us. Let us take a look at some of his hit men. Please understand that this is by no means a complete list:

1 . Trouble –things that disturb
1 . Misery- wretchedly deficient, causing extreme discomfort
3 . Distress-misfortunes, suffering great need
4 . Pain-suffering of body or mind
5 . Depression-to experience a time of low-

ness
6 . Oppression-persecute or to weight down
7 . Worry-feeling of anxiety (anxiety-uneasiness usually over an expected misfortune)
8 . Tribulations-suffering from oppression
9 . Heartache- anguish of mind (anguish-extreme pain or distress of the mind)
10 . Enslavement-things that makes one a slave
11 . Fear-false evidence which appears real
12 . Lust-intense longing for things off limits
13 . Temptation- something that tempts or appeals to your affections instead of Christ
14 . Spiritual coldness- leaving your first love
15 . Slothfulness-indolence, lazy, idleness
16 . Apathy-lack of emotion or interest
17 . Egomania-extremely self-centered
18 . Harassment-worry and impede (an enemy) by repeated raids, to annoy continually
19 . Torment-extreme pain or anguish or a source of pain likened unto it.
20 . Too busy-this is last on my list, but Satan places it first on his list when dealing with today's Christians.

Every attack that Satan makes on a believer, he wants to make the life of that dear soul so miserable that, he/she forgets that the Lord ever lived. Satan knows how to apply pressure to our lives, but he seems to have forgotten that the Lord is in our lives. Maybe he hasn't forgotten, that is the main reason he is so relentless in his pursuit to over throw us.

When Mr. Trouble makes his attack in your life, you make sure that you don't let him point out other people as the cause of your problem. This is one of his number one tactics. He loves to use people to help intensify the problems in our lives. You may recall the attitudes of Job's comforters. They came, supposing to encourage Job, but they were more successful at adding to his misery. Satan has been very successful in getting people to pull one another down. He delights in that because it allows his work to go forth with the appearance of a human problem, but in the end it yields devilish results.

Job's so called comforters harassed him so in speculating his guilt until they were successful in getting him to do something that Satan had failed to get him to do and that is to speak amiss concerning God. In the end Job had to put his hand over his mouth because he knew that he had talked too much in response to the foolish accusations his friends had made.

Satan was out of the picture in a sense, but in reality he was the main culprit in what was going on. Those so-called comforters were being influenced by Satan's way of thinking. That is why they were able to discourage rather than encourage Job. They were influenced to hurt him, but in the end, they had to have Job to pray for them before God could bless them again.

Thank God that Job was in a position to pray for the ones that had harassed him and tormented him with words. When Job was able Job's power to pray for the ones that had attacked his character, speaks well of the God in Job. It demonstrates how well God can hold his children together even when they are under attack. It makes clear the meaning of Psalms 34:19. We are assured by that verse that regardless to the afflicting circumstances, we are sure to be delivered out of them all.

"Many are the afflictions of the righteous: but the LORD delivereth him out of them all."- Ps 34:19

Meditating on all in this verse should increase faith to some fainting heart. We can believe that God's all means exactly all. We can take heart when we are under attack, knowing that the outcome works in our favor and are made better in the end.

GOOD MEN DO
SUFFER BAD THINGS

In the second chapter of Job, we see that being good does not immune us from trouble. After Satan could not get Job to defy or curse God by taking Job's livestock and his children, He then returned with another plan. This plan, he was sure, would work because it would hit where it hurts the most.

> *"Well, have you noticed my servant Job?" the Lord asked. "He is the finest man in all the earth-a good man who fears God and turns away from all evil. And he has kept his faith in me despite the fact that you persuaded me to let you harm him without any cause."- Job 2:3 TLB*

No greater testimony could be given in regards to a man than the one the Lord gave concerning Job. He gave Job credit for being a fine man; Job was tops in the earth. God also mentioned the steadfastness of Job's faith while under fire. God's testimony concerning Job, more than likely, stirred Satan the more because he wanted a piece of Job. Although Satan is known for his persistence, he also knows when he has met with a soldier that is unwilling to give in to his pressure. Now, when Satan makes that assessment, he always has another game plan.

God's question upon his return was the same as it had been previously. "From whence comest thou? Has thou considered my servant Job?" Satan again fulfills his role as an accuser. However, this time he says Job's skin is the only thing that he has left, and if his skin was touched he would curse God to His face.

> *"Skin for skin," Satan replied. "A man will give anything to save his life. Touch his body with sickness, and he will curse you to your face!"- Job 2:4 TLB*

Satan is selfish; therefore, he thinks that everyone else is selfish. We know that selfish people look out for number one first. Satan seemingly disregarded the assessment that God made of Job's characteristics because he believed that Job had a hidden agenda. He believed that if Job's body was touched, something other than uprightness would definitely come out.

Satan's fall from heaven further convinced him that all men are subject to fall no matter how holy they are. In today's phraseology we say, "Everybody has a price; simply find out his price and buy him". Satan felt obligated to make sure that it happened in Job's life. I suppose we could be sympathetic with

Satan. If we care to, we can clearly see his view point as an accuser. Some of the accusations he raises against us are true and it may be hard for him to see why his mistake got him kicked out of heaven, and the human race continually makes mistakes and they are on their way to heaven. That might be hard for him to swallow.

It has to be mind boggling to Satan to see us make mistakes and God forgives us. He made a mistake and lost his heavenly home. Since he can't punish God for what happened, he continually seeks to make us pay. He will go to any length to inflict hurt and harm upon anyone that chooses to live a godly life.

I am sure Satan has to take it personally when one steps out from a sinning world to devote his or her life to the Master. Our choosing to live holy lives we reflects Satan's loss and what we have gained. So then it is great mystery why Satan releases his anger upon the lives of those who honor the Lord with holy living. He keeps his army fired up and ready to fight against everyone who has a desire to follow the Lord. Their assignment is to turn them around by whatever means possible, and it doesn't matter how long it takes to accomplish the task; he is willing to keep on until they give up and turn.

I say to every reader, if you hold to the Lord's unchanging hand, the going might get rough, but you will surely make it because you are tough in Jesus, and you are more than a conqueror. You may look like a loser; nevertheless, you are a winner. You are well protected and as long as you desire Jesus, He desires to provide you with His divine presence and protection.

When Job withstood Satan's first bombardment, Satan knew then that he needed to get some of Job's skin. And with God's permission, Satan smote Job from his crown to the soles of his feet. From all historical accounts, Job was in a seemingly unbearable condition. However, he maintained his loyalty to God. In fact, he was so steadfast that even his wife was moved to try and help Satan accomplish what he thought Job would have done long before his wife suggested it. He depends so heavily on human help; as a matter of fact, I dare say carnality is seventy-five percent of his help, and were it not for the help of humans, he'd be almost out of business. He loves to have those close to us speak in support of what he seeks to do. People that are close to us sometimes make suggestions that appear to be genuine concern, only to discover they were Satan's thoughts designed to defeat what our purpose and resolve. I assert this with confidence because it happened to Jesus. One of His own disciples allowed Satan to speak through him in the guise of concern.

"From that time forth began Jesus to shew unto his disciples, how that he must go unto Jerusalem, and suffer many things of the elders and chief priests and scribes, and be killed, and be raised again the third day.

22 Then Peter took him, and began to rebuke him, saying, Be it far from thee, Lord: this shall not be unto thee.

> ***23 But he turned, and said unto Peter, Get thee behind me, Satan: thou art an offence unto me: for thou savourest not the things that be of God, but those that be of men."-Matt 16:21-23***

It wasn't that Peter didn't love the Lord. The fact is that Peter was being used by the Lord's enemy without even realizing it.

I recall the many words of advice given to me when the word got out that I was entering into full time ministry. They were, no doubt, concerned about my welfare, but I was concerned about the call of God upon my life and about His kingdom coming and His will being done in me. I am thankful that the Lord helped me not to give in to the words of those well meaning people. I feel that had I done so, I would not be where I am today; I would not know the power of God as I do; and I wouldn't have the revelation knowledge that I have.

Here is a known fact; Satan will use whoever is available no matter how closely or remotely they are connected to us. In fact, the only guaranteed One not to be used by Satan is to our Lord and Savior Jesus Christ. You can safely give Him complete authority over your life.

This is only another confirmation that living godly does not remove one from Satan's hit list; but rather, it puts one at the top of his list. The better we live, and the more we worship and praise the Lord, the more it angers the devil because our worship of God brings back old memories. It reminds Satan of the great pleasure God receives when worship is directed to Him. The heart of God is thrilled by the worship of His children; it is the one thing that gratifies Him for the sacrifice He made to redeem us from sin.

I believe that it was the element of satisfaction that God expressed when receiving worship from His people that got Satan in trouble. Upon seeing God's reaction to worship, it no doubt made him feel that he should be receiving some of the credit. That is the thing that got Satan in trouble. Since he could not share in the receiving of worship, he decided that he would go all out to prevent men from worshiping. He attempts to stop us from worshiping by making our lives so miserable that we lose our desire to worship. Satan hopes that the trouble he brings upon us will leave us so confused and hurt that we are ready to charge God foolishly and withhold our worship.

If you really want to upset the devil, just go ahead and offer God praise and worship regardless to your present circumstances because the Lord is worthy of all honor and praise. In addition to God's worthiness, when we forget about ourselves and concentrate on the Lord and worship Him we send hell a message. That message is, out of all the unpleasant things that may be happening to me, I yet have praise. I can yet worship my Lord in spite of what I am going through.

The Lord made His children tough when He filled them with His Spirit. We are nobody's push over. We are given His divine nature. We are equipped to handle life's difficulties by His indwelling Holy Spirit. The Lord stands with us and stands up in us.

Satan attempts to use life's difficulties to curtail the praises that are due the Lord. He wants to make everybody a quitter because he is a quitter. He tries to make the journey to heaven sound impossible. But why should we consider him? Since he was there and would not stay, why should we let him make us think we cannot make it? Since he is so bothered by our love and relationship with the Lord, Satan has no other choice but to try and make life miserable for us. He hopes that by doing so, we will give up and throw in the towel and call it quits. However, believers are not known for drawing back, but they are known for believing unto the end.

"But we are not of them who draw back unto perdition; but of them that believe to the saving of the soul."- Heb 10:39

If Job had been a person given to the drawback spirit, it would have, no doubt, taken control of him when he heard the plea of his sympathetic wife calling for him to curse God and die. When Satan is on our case one of the last things we need is human sympathy because it tends to make us feel sorry for ourselves more than it does anything else.

Along with all the trouble Satan stirs up, we are passing through a foreign land trying to get home. Some foreigners can be very hostile toward strangers. However, we are only treated as strangers when we cleave to the laws of our God. We will find acceptance from the god of this world if we choose to walk contrary to the Word. The world wants us to adapt to this present system so that we will lose track on where we are going.

> *"And take heed to yourselves, lest at any time your hearts be overcharged with surfeiting, and drunkenness, and cares of this life, and so that day come upon you unawares."-* Luke 21:34

It pleases the enemy to no end when he succeeds in getting us to fall in love with this world and lose sight on our eternal destiny. Satan feels that every soul that he can get drunk on the affairs of this world, he will be one less on the road for heaven.

> *"Dearly beloved, I beseech you as strangers and pilgrims, abstain from fleshly lusts, which war against the soul;"-* 1 Peter 2:11

When we combine all that Satan does directly and all that he does to us through the media of the world and the flesh, it is clear to us that good men do suffer bad things. Not all of us know how to handle it; and some completely lose out while others recover.

> *"Truly God is good to Israel, even to such as are of a clean heart.*
>
> *2 But as for me, my feet were almost gone; my steps had well nigh slipped.*

3 For I was envious at the foolish, when I saw the prosperity of the wicked.

4 For there are no bands in their death: but their strength is firm.

5 They are not in trouble as other men; neither are they plagued like other men."
- Ps 73:1-5

However, there is no out of this world reward for the wicked. Whatever they get in this life equals the sum total of what they have to look forward to. That is another reason why we should not seek to take from the world the things that they depend on for happiness and pleasure. We should not mind seeing them have some of the things that Christians no longer need for fulfillment.

It seems to me that those who come into the church from a rough background seem to survive hard times much better than those who are accustomed to a life of ease. I suppose that is understandable because we are creatures of habit, and change throws us out of balance. When one has known life's ups and downs before becoming a Christian that soul is really prepared for the many challenges Christian life will offers. If pressure brings out the best in us, we are in the right arena to demonstrate what we are made of. Trouble is known to polish and bring out of us what God has put in us. There seems to be no other way to show God's greatness than allowing trouble to come upon His believing children. The trouble maker hopes to defeat us while hurting and shaming our God but remember God takes what Satan meant for harm and makes it work for our good. When we hang tough, it allows God to turn things around and make them work for our good as long as we love Him.

"If thou faint in the day of adversity, thy strength is small."- Prov 24:10

When we hang tough, it allows God to turn things around and make them work for our good as long as we love Him.

"And we know that all things work together for good to them that love God, to them who are the called according to his purpose." - Rom 8:28

Hanging tough is our badge of identification. We are known for our ability to outlast our troubles, we count difficulties as a part of the Christian walk, and we learn to prepare for the heat that comes.

"If thou faint in the day of adversity, thy strength is small."- Prov 24:10

The Christian walk comes with much opposition, and if you are reluctant to do battle, you are in the wrong army. Practice the drill. "In this warfare, you don't have to go looking for trouble, just keep living according to the Word of God, and trouble will seek you out."

"If thou faint in the day of adversity, thy strength is small."- Prov 24:10

"Fight the good fight of faith, lay hold on eternal life, whereunto thou art also called, and hast professed a good profession before many witnesses."- 1 Tim 6:12

This war is called a good fight; it is a good fight because of the good benefits that follow a successful battle. You can see that Job had the right spirit while facing his predicament. His focus seemed to have been more on God than it was on what he had lost. Anytime one can focus like that, there is absolutely nothing the enemy can do to rob him of his relationship with the Lord. And may I reiterate, "We are in an army that is presently under siege but thanks be to God, we are a well-equipped army." We are an army that is following the WORLD'S GREATEST LEADER—one that has never lost a battle, one who cannot lose one who knows the end from the beginning and everything in between a leader that has all power in His hand!!! Go on and Crown Him With Hallelujah!!!

Although contrary winds may blow upon your life, you are yet more than a conqueror. I didn't say that you look like a conqueror; I said that you are more than a conqueror because God has not stopped giving pinnacle endings similar to the one He gave Job.

51

Job received double for his troubles, and in the end it was Job that rejoiced, rather than Satan-the trouble maker.

"Then, when Job prayed for his friends, the Lord restored his wealth and happiness! In fact, the Lord gave him twice as much as before!

11 Then all of his brothers, sisters, and former friends arrived and feasted with him in his home, consoling him for all his sorrow and comforting him because of all the trials the Lord had brought upon him. And each of them brought him a gift of money and a gold ring.

12 So the Lord blessed Job at the end of his life more than at the beginning. For now he had 14,000 sheep, 6,000 camels, 1,000 teams of oxen, and 1,000 female donkeys."- Job 42:10 -12 TLB

The spirit and truth of Romans 8:28 came alive in Job's life, and it will come alive in the lives of all whose trust is in the Lord. Nevertheless, while we are waiting for the fulfillment of God's word, we need to speak about what we believe, and not what we see. Faith in God's promises is our shield equipment. Believing and speaking the Word of God, substantiates our hoped for victory and protects against fiery darts of doubt and unbelief. Unwavering faith is the victory that overcomes the world. Throughout biblical experiences, this weapon has proven to be unchanging source of power. While what we see might change many times right before our very eyes, we can be sure that the Word of the Lord abides forever.

"For ever, O LORD, thy word is settled in heaven."- Ps 119:89

Since God's Word is already settled in heaven, we need to get it settled in us because it is the Word that settles every issue that the enemy attempts to raise.

Even good men must rely on the Word of God to prevent the enemy from gaining the upper hand in their affairs. Daniel lived well and treated others with the utmost respect; however, his good practice landed him in a den of lions where his faith equipment was tested. His faith worked; the LORD stood with him and brought him out unharmed. Daniel's inconvenience blessed him to represent and to present God in such a way that it incited the king to issue a decree of worship in favor of Daniel and his God.

"Then king Darius wrote unto all people, nations, and languages, that dwell in all the earth; Peace be multiplied unto you.

26 I make a decree, That in every dominion of my kingdom men tremble and fear before the God of Daniel: for he is the living God, and stedfast for ever, and his kingdom that which shall not be destroyed, and his dominion shall be even unto the end.

27 He delivereth and rescueth, and he worketh signs and wonders in heaven and in earth, who hath delivered Daniel from the power of the lions."- Dan 6:25-27

The barbarity of putting a good man in a lion's den just for praying, no doubt, sounds ludicrous. However, good men do suffer cruel and unjust penalties, especially at the hand of those who are evil. Men who are under the influence of Satan are known to behave in a satanic manner like Satan's. As these ungodly men were angered by Daniel's praying so Satan is angered by the prayers of all of God's saints, and will do anything within his power to stop all praying.

The move to shut down every prayer meeting is a top priority for the evil one because the prayers of the righteous bombard the kingdom of hell with a powerful war cry, "We're going to tear your kingdom down." Satan would rather see us doing anything other than praying, he knows that praying brings God into what is going on and he wants nothing to do with God; therefore, he feels that he must stop all praying.

We can be sure that our continued praying gives our God an opportunity to glorify Himself. Just think if the enemies could have stopped Daniel from praying, God would not have been glorified in the manner that He was. The Babylonian kingdom was ruled by that ungodly ruler at a time when God's own people were so cast down within themselves they could no longer sing God's praise in a strange land. But Daniel's trust brought glory to God. And verily I say unto you, those captured souls from Judah were ecstatic to be exhorted to Praise their God again. Therefore, the next time you feel unduly put upon and think that your lifestyle is so holy before God, that nothing but good should come your way. Please rebuke that attitude and ask God to show you His plan in your time of difficulty because the enemy would take such a thought and cause you to blame God when you are attacked, thereby giving assistance to what the devil is doing. He would like for us to feel that we deserve better since we have lived so pure and holy. After all should not blessings follow good behavior? This is the kind" spirit we humans demonstrate, but the reality of it all is good men do suffer bad things just as evil men are sometimes blessed greatly.

Samuel was another good man whose heart was made to bleed by the not-so-good lifestyles of his sons. This has been the test of many good men and women down through the years. While we were busy serving God and His people, our sons and daughters were busy practicing what we preached against. Some ministers suffered more than others because some thought as much as they taught their children and as holy as they walked before them, there would be no way their children would not live right. But when they found out differently, they were so devastated that their nights became long, lonesome, fearful and frightening. However, they learned that bad things do happen to good people. I can not think of anything worse than to losing your own children to a world of destruction. No doubt, the good man Samuel suffered; and likewise, have many others suffered, and many more will suffer at the sight of lost children. Only eternity will reveal the many tears that have been shed in secret by good men because of the misbehavior of their children.

"Then all the elders of Israel gathered themselves together, and came to Samuel unto Ramah,

5 And said unto him, Behold, thou art old, and thy sons walk not in thy ways: now make us a king to judge us like all the nations."- 1 Sam 8:4-5

Breaking up homes and families has always been high among Satan's top priorities. The home and the church are ordained of God as dispensaries of love—place where love is taught and demonstrated and engraved in children's minds as the only good and wise way to live. So this hater of all love would rather divide homes, and churches and schools and pollute children than build another tavern. It thrills him to no end to see good men make the sacrifice to bring up godly children, only to see them become rebellious children. Oh, he is deliriously happy when he sees children resenting the lifestyle of the parents and complaining of strictness. Satan gets busy making plans to acquaint them with all the glamour he has for them, inviting them to take a trip to the far country looking for excitement. "You're young." "You can't live like your old-fashioned parents." "Have some fun." "See some of the world." "Let me show you how to live." Satan knows, if he can get them away from the influence of their godly parent, he stands a good chance of killing them in their sins.

I would like to say to all parents with wayward children: just keep praying because God never stops caring for even the prodigal.

We have God's Word to help us to understand that bad things do happen to good men but these happenings will not go unnoticed by God. In His own due time, He is sure to turn things around for the good of His people. Another use for your faith is to apply it full strength when the going gets rough and the hills are hard to climb. This is not a sign that the Lord has departed from His people. Neither does it mean that we are losing the battle; it just means that God's glory will shine even brighter when He shows up in our difficulties. The greater the opposition, the greater the triumph.

TROUBLE IS
A GOOD TIME TO KNOW
THE LORD

Some lessons we learn late, and there are some we can manage without ever learning. But when it comes to trouble and knowing the Lord, we are much better off when we know the Lord in advance because nothing seems to reveal our place in God like trouble. Whether or not we are anchored in Jesus, we can be sure that trouble will come and trouble will reveal what we have done with our allotted time. Trouble will reveal whether or not we have spent our time in prayer and devotion or in fruitless pleasure. This is not to say that prayer and devotion would keep trouble from rising, but it would sure keep us from falling.

TROUBLE IS A DEFECT CORRECTOR

After reading the book of Job in its entirety, we can see that many of Job's views were brought to light. This never would have happened had it not been for the troubles he suffered. To the true child of God, trouble is a blessing in disguise; its true value is hidden like diamond in coal, but by and by, the end results of our sufferings, will surely shine forth.

Job 42:5 I have heard of thee by the hearing of the ear: but now mine eye seeth thee. KJV

Job could not utter these profound words until after he had gone through the channels of suffering. Job's troubles had revealed to him a clearer picture of himself; but best of all, it had revealed the God that he loved.

This is another reason we can call trouble a blessing in disguise because of the increased knowledge of the power of God to deliver us from trouble or from being in trouble.

Having this knowledge, we are able to rejoice or count ourselves blessed when we are allowed to encounter difficulties, because in the end, out troubles are sure to work for our good.

"And not only so, but we glory in tribulations also: knowing that tribulation worketh patience; - (Rom 5:3)

Paul said that we glory in tribulations. Choosing one of the many meanings of the word "glory," the one that stands out here to me is the one that means "boast." This is not speaking of one boasting in oneself, but exulting in trouble. That, resting in the assurance that one is standing in the safety of God's Word. Trouble will put a choke chain around our necks if our standing with God is uncertain. But if we are standing in the safety zone, trouble is nothing more than a cause for rejoicing or boasting.

"My soul shall make her boast in the LORD: the humble shall hear thereof, and be glad."
- Ps 34:2

"In God we boast all the day long, and praise thy name for ever. Selah"- Ps 44:8

"Blessed is the man that endureth temptation: for when he is tried, he shall receive the crown of life, which the Lord hath promised to them that love him. - James 1:12

When we have been through something serious, we find it easy to boast of God's goodness and mighty deliverance. In fact, that is what our testimony service is supposed to be devoted to. It should be a time for the children of God to boast about the Lord's doings and our fresh daily walk with Him. Looking at it from the Scripture and from personal observation, it appears that trouble really gives us something to declare. Trouble also gives us occasion

61

to see-God in us. We see the Lord as merciful and true to His word, and we see ourselves as needing to know Him better. There are some things about God that only trouble will provoke us to seek because we are not, as a whole, known to go too far or move too fast without a push. Trouble, then, can be thought of as that necessary push.

When God allows trials to come upon us, they are not for Him to discover what's in us, but rather they are for us to learn what is there or what needs to be there that is not already there—what equipment we have, what equipment we need, what necessary equipment is long overdue. Paul spoke about "*tribulation worketh patience*;" Notice the word "*worketh*." We are taught that a word with the "*eth*" ending means continued progress. That being true, tribulation or trouble keeps on working to produce patience. We need to remember that fact so that the next time we request prayer for patience, we must remember that we are inviting more trouble into our lives because it is trouble that keeps working patience.

And as far as I know, none of us were born with forbearance. However, the fire can and will burn away the dross so that patience can have her perfect work in us.

"That the trial of your faith, being much more precious than of gold that perisheth, though it be tried with fire, might be found unto praise and honour and glory at the appearing of Jesus Christ:"-(1 Peter 1:7)

"Blessed is the man that endureth temptation: for when he is tried, he shall receive the crown of life, which the Lord hath promised to them that love him"- James 1:12

It will also determine how long we must stay in a given situation. There is nothing more distasteful than going through with the wrong attitude and coming out without the right results. Having to go back through with hopes of learning this time around is not fun; but if we don't learn the first time, there is always the second, third, fourth, and "et cetera" time.

1 Peter 4:1 Forasmuch then as Christ hath suffered for us in the flesh, arm yourselves likewise with the same mind: for he that hath suffered in the flesh hath ceased from sin;

2 That he no longer should live the rest of his time in the flesh to the lusts of men, but to the will of God. KJV

Satan seems to have thought that trouble would obviously make Job bitter enough to curse God to His face. It is true that some people are so unprepared for trouble that once it hits; they are known to revert to their past habits, as a way of getting back at God. Not everyone comes out of trouble with growth. Some come out with gripes; and some don't even make it through. Those that experience a fresh relationship with God while encountering trouble are known to grow sweeter. But those that view trouble as a raw deal will have a difficult time finding sweetness.

One of the passages we so often quote:

"For his anger endureth but a moment; in his favour is life: weeping may endure for a night, but joy cometh in the morning."
- Ps 30:5

We can see that tears are replaced with joy after we endure the night. This kind of expectancy gives us the necessary ingredients to sweetness.

I am reminded of the inscription that once appeared on the bottle of Real Lemon Juice: "We squeeze so you can pour." It can be said that the Lord allows the enemy to squeeze so that the Lord can pour us out as a blessing to many others. Our bitter experiences prepare us to be a sweet blessing to others that are encountering trouble; they are encouraged by the sweet testimony of our deliverance.

Ps 30:11 Thou hast turned for me my mourning into dancing: thou hast put off my sackcloth, and girded me with gladness; KJV

The difference we should be able to see is in the way we view God in light of what is happening to us. When we can be sure that passing the night of weeping will be replaced with morning joy, it makes the night much easier or it builds our hope so high we hardly notice the pain that the night brought. When one can go from mourning to dancing and from sack-cloth to gladness, he has more to look forward to than he has to look back on.

TROUBLE A TRAINING COURSE SEREVICE

You may notice in the Bible, many, if not all, who did great works for he Lord had much training in the school of opposition. That's because trouble is known to either bring out the best or the worst of a person. When the best is brought out, they are best equipped for the Lord's service. It is a fact that none of us have to solicit the trouble that precedes the job; it just seems to be included according to the job to be done.

It was impossible for Joseph to know that his dreams which caused so much friction in his home were part of a training course that would equip him to run a country. And when his parents along with his brothers rejected his dreams, he could see that he was surrounded by all- out opposition.

To make a bad situation worse, his brothers sold him. Allow me to say it this way, **his brothers sent him off to school.** After all, school is where one goes to prepare for one's life work, isn't it? What appeared to be the end for Joseph was only the beginning. What seemed to be a tragedy turned out to be a triumph for all of God's children?

In a very short time, Joseph learned some valuable lessons at the "University of Trouble." All of his professors were well-qualified to present each needed lesson. However, his home study course had somewhat prepared him for what to expect in Egypt. He no doubt understood that if his own brothers could be as cruel as they were at home, he should not expect any special favor from the people in Egypt. It is always a head start when one faces life's difficulties expecting the worse but knowing what to do when things get better.

In addition to the secular education Joseph received at home, God had equipped him for his tenure in Egypt. Many times we have read in the biographies of Joseph, Moses, David and even King Saul that they were "goodly" to look upon. This means they possessed a choice countenance, easy to look upon, spirited eyes reflecting a lively soul, and an obedient demeanor as though always attuned to God. A person of God could just glance at him and see the Spirit of the Living God at work. This is the God given armor/equipment he took into idolatrous Egypt. But in this goodly soul, was the fear of the only Almighty God. His daily meditation may well have been: "With God on my side, I can do this."

His experience between home and where he spent the remainder of his life reveals a lesson that all men can profit from. That is, brothers will sell you and lie about what really happened. They will sell you even if they don't get very much for you; they feel that selling you would get rid of you forever. The spirit of selling a brother is very much alive today, and price is not a factor, they just want to get free of your spiritual presence.

Gen 37:27 Come, and let us sell him to the Ishmeelites, and let not our hand be upon him; for he is our brother and our flesh. And his brethren were content. KJV

So consider this principle: If you are sold by your brothers, it could be that they are sending you off to school to prepare for that position you said you wanted, or that service you wanted so badly to render for the betterment of God's people and the glory of our great King. I know it doesn't feel good knowing that brothers would sell you, but it is sometimes part of the course that leads to great success. Notwithstanding, allowing the bad things others do to us to harbor bitterness can tarnish the goodly equipment with which God has so lovingly fitted us, causing us to hold grudges, retaliate or get even next time we see our offender. Two wrongs have never equaled a right.

Joseph's life in Egypt started off on a high note; he found favor with his master because of the "goodly" character/equipment God gave him. God prospered him in whatever he did because he remembered God. Keep in mind that God's blessings will soften the blows of trouble in our lives because we are more focused on the good things that God is doing than we are on the evil that is happening to us.

Since Satan is a trouble maker and hates to see anyone honor God and fare well, he brought in another teacher to present a lesson that most men have been known to fail. Nevertheless, with Joseph it was just a matter of remembering God's rules for maintaining the equipment. *__While playing by the rules attracts problems, it always brings solution and triumph.__*

Gen 39:7 And it came to pass after these things, that his master's wife cast her eyes upon Joseph; and she said, Lie with me.

8 But he refused, and said unto his master's wife, Behold, my master wotteth not what is with me in the house, and he hath committed all that he hath to my hand;

9 There is none greater in this house than I; neither hath he kept back any thing from me but thee, because thou art his wife: how then can I do this great wickedness, and sin against God?

10 And it came to pass, as she spake to Joseph day by day, that he hearkened not unto her, to lie by her, or to be with her. KJV

Joseph passed that course with excellent grades. In fact, his G.P.A. was 4.0. To get the position for which he was training his grades had to be impeccable. After successfully mastering one of the university's most difficult courses, he was falsely accused. This lie led to his being assigned to Egyptian dungeon to further his education.

Knowing that the Lord is with us regardless of our present trial takes away much of the hurt and conditions us to hang on in there. Thank God that there is a place in Him that takes much of the pain out of trouble; that takes the heat out of the flame; that lightens the weight of the cross and takes the bite out of the lions' mouth, and lands us safely on the only boat that is floating. Selah!! Is there any god, besides our God?? No, I know not any.

I am sure that prison was no picnic for Joseph, but knowing the Lord made life bearable. The knowledge of His abiding presence gives consolation in whatever we are doing Teachers tend to assess "goodly" students, differently from the other students. Although Joseph was a prisoner, he was looked upon differently because of this special equipment he wore. The Lord was with him and caused whatever he did to prosper.

Gen 39:21 But the LORD was with Joseph, and shewed him mercy, and gave him favour in the sight of the keeper of the prison.

22 And the keeper of the prison committed to Joseph's hand all the prisoners that were in the prison; and whatsoever they did there, he was the doer of it.

23 The keeper of the prison looked not to any thing that was under his hand; because the LORD was with him, and that which he did, the LORD made it to prosper. KJV

Knowing the Lord, we experience tremendous growth from the troubles that try us. Instead of going under, we go over. It is not the predicament that makes the difference in our lives, it is the attitude that we have toward the predicament. Joseph was able to maintain his focus; therefore, he was successful in enduring this particular course. To maintain focus one must be able to project and perceive a good outcome from what he is presently suffering—must perceive joy set before. This was the kind of focus that aided Jesus in enduring the cross. It was the joy of what would be accomplished that sustained Him. This is the kind of focus that will also sustain us. What we need to do is keep our eyes on Jesus, no matter how dark our night or day becomes; we must keep our eyes on the Master. Jesus is our light in darkness; He is our hope for tomorrow and our shelter in the time of a storm. If the storm succeeds in getting us to take our eyes off Jesus, we can be sure that we are going to sink, so no matter how the winds blows and the mountains crumble or whatever other noise is made, let us keep our eyes fixed on Jesus and He is sure to see us through.

Heb 12:2 Looking unto Jesus the author and finisher of our faith; who for the joy that was set before him endured the cross, despising the shame, and is set down at the right hand of the throne of God.

3 For consider him that endured such contradiction of sinners against himself, lest ye be wearied and faint in your minds. KJV

Satan would like for every breeze of trouble to seem like a hurricane and every bolt of noise to seem like an earthquake. Because fear is one of his best weapons, it will neutralize our faith; it is impossible to fear and have faith at the same time. Therefore, Satan seeks to blow everything out of proportion with hopes of filling us with trepidation.

When God is in control in our lives, we can be sure we will be at the right place at the right time. It was necessary for Joseph to be put in prison. In prison, (his third course of study) his special qualifications were discovered. Joseph had an encounter with the men that had big house connections. He did not get where he was going right away, but after patience had had her perfect work, in due time it came to pass. The chief butler's failure to remember Joseph was not an accident. The time for his rise to the next level had not come, and God wanted him good and ready to occupy the position He himself was creating for Joseph at the top.

This reminds me of an enquiry made by one of my fellow pastor's years ago. He wanted to know how long it took me before my congregation commenced to grow. I speculated for him the time, but I questioned him by asking him would he like for God to give him 100 followers while he was only able to care for 10 or would he rather grow to the level that he could care for more before they were added? The point is, God has a time frame (a season) that governs His release of blessings. He gives us time to grow up before He overloads us with what He has in store for us. That is why trouble is known to precede blessings; they come to test our ability to carry on without dipping our hands in God's glory.

God has no problem loading us with blessings once we have successfully passed our courses taught by life's difficulties, troubles, hardships and pain. Therefore, we should not be so quick to push the panic button; we just might be enrolled in the only course that prepares us for our next miracle.

There is nothing more devastating than to reach the pinnacle of so-called success without proper preparation. It is sad but true, too many have already run that course and failed to comprehend the real meaning. That is why we are seeing so many federal investigations in high places and constant failures among church leaderships. They attained their offices either too soon or too unprepared, or they climbed up the wrong way, without successfully passing the required courses. And once they get there unprepared, they make shipwreck of the position. There is nowhere to go but down when one is not qualified to stay on top. This is one school that you cannot skip, cheat or cut corners on and come out on top, you must stay the course and pass with good grades or it will be revealed later in embarrassing circumstances. If they had studied well at the "University of Trouble," they would have had the character to maintain a consistent life.

The high tuition of the school of trouble makes one think before getting involved with some sex crazy woman or man. The person that has paid to be exalted is not quick to sacrifice all that he has invested just for a moment of pleasure.

By Joseph having contact with the chief butler—his link to the high calling of God—he was called forth out of the iron furnace. Although Joseph had not come to Egypt to be prime minister, he was, nonetheless, the man best qualified for the job. Trouble had conditioned him and God had positioned him to be at the right place at the right time.

I am reminded of the words of a song: "When you are tempted to fret or complain, just think of His goodness to you." Those who really know the Lord, have much more to be thankful for than they have to complain over.

We have already established the fact that none of us is privileged to specify when or how or what kind of trouble we prefer. Actually, we know that if we live godly, trouble is going to come. Therefore, let us spend our time getting to know the Lord better so that when trouble does come, our anchor will be in the Lord. The man who does not know the Lord in distressful situations turns to alcohol, drugs, food, squandering, or any other act of stupidity he can think of for a measure of relief. Conversely, the man who really knows the Lord, stands ready and willing to offer the Lord another praise *Hab 3:17 Although the fig tree shall not blossom, neither shall fruit be in the vines; the labour of the olive shall fail, and the fields shall yield no meat; the flock shall be cut off from the fold, and there shall be no herd in the stalls:*

18 Yet I will rejoice in the LORD, I will joy in the God of my salvation. KJV

When we really love the Lord, we gladly take all conditional clauses out of our relationship with Him because we know He is well able to see us through. His providential record is flawless when it comes to taking good care of His children. This fact is verified throughout both Testaments.

Seeking the Lord in the time of trouble just happens to be the continuation of a pattern one has set during the time of peace. The time of trouble is no time to start trying to know Him. This matter should begin shortly after we are introduced to Him by the Holy Ghost. We need to start seeking His presence through being consistent in prayer. Herein we are assured of gaining a better relationship with Him. The arrival of trouble only testifies that we have made wise use of our time and are now prepared to be tested.

IIChron. 20:3 And Jehoshaphat feared, and set himself to seek the LORD, and proclaimed a fast throughout all Judah. KJV

Thank God, he didn't push the panic button; in stead, he sought the Lord and encouraged others to do the same. The number of enemies or the size of a problem should not prevent us from doing what we do best-that is seeking the Lord. Whatever the problem is, we have access the power supply. If we seek Him, we will find Him and He will hear and answer.

2 Chron 20:5 And Jehoshaphat stood in the congregation of Judah and Jerusalem, in the house of the LORD, before the new court,

6 And said, O LORD God of our fathers, art not thou God in heaven? and rulest not thou over all the kingdoms of the heathen? and in thine hand is there not power and might, so that none is able to withstand thee? KJV

You can tell from Jehoshaphat's prayer that it wasn't the first time he had prayed and that he knew to whom he was talking.

2 Chron 20:6 And said, O LORD God of our fathers, art not thou God in heaven? and rulest not thou over all the kingdoms of the heathen? and in thine hand is there not power and might, so that none is able to withstand thee? KJV

In other words, when his troubles came, he already knew where to turn and how to turn to Him.

Jehoshaphat prayed and confessed what God's word had said, and then God sent a messenger to encourage the hearts of His people. When we do what we know to, we can always expect God to give us a word to sustain us in the time of opposition. Hearing God's word will cause our hearts to rest in confidence.

2 Chron 20:15 And he said, Hearken ye, all Judah, and ye inhabitants of Jerusalem, and thou king Jehoshaphat, Thus saith the LORD unto you, Be not afraid nor dismayed by reason of this great multitude; for the battle is not yours, but God's. KJV

2 Chron 20:17 Ye shall not need to fight in this battle: set yourselves, stand ye still, and see the salvation of the LORD with you, O Judah and Jerusalem: fear not, nor be dismayed; to morrow go out against them: for the LORD will be with you. KJV

It is a good thing to know the Lord. If we do not know Him, our troubles will take us down for the count. Knowing Him allows us to seek Him, and when we seek Him, it allows Him to take His active role in our affairs. After addressing God the way Jehoshaphat did, there was no fear of God standing back to watch the enemy overpower His people. Faith conquered fear!

If you have a record of calling upon Him when things are well, just remember, He is the same God when things are not so well. Since He does not change, it would be best to acquaint yourself with Him in the time of peace, and you would have little difficulty calling upon Him in the times of trouble. Our relationship with God is the only license God needs to get involved in our troubles. The Word of God came to Jehoshaphat, "for the battle is not yours, but God's." This is the kind of knowledge that comes through knowing the Lord in a very personal way.

If you are the Lord's, that situation you are facing today, is His problem. One cannot separate himself from his problems and neither can our problems separate us from God. Therefore, when you are tempted to walk the floor rather than go to bed and sleep, just remember that you are the Lord's responsibility, and if you are in trouble, so is He because you are His property. We just need to turn it over to Him and get our rest because He works around the clock. He never slumbers, and neither does He sleep. And since we belong to Him, He doesn't mind us sleeping while He keeps watch over us. This advice, of course, is for victorious believers. How does one become a victorious believer? Here is the key:

Let us take a look at some of the key things that lead to victory:

1 . Prayer (vs. 5-13)
2 . The Word of God (vs. 14-17)
3 . Praise and worship (vs. 18-19)
4 . Exhortation (vs. 20)
5 . Participation (vs.21-22).

Again I say, it always confounds the enemy when one is able to offer praise in the face of great odds. Satan has said that no one can maintain his or her relationship with God in the thick of trouble. But when we pray right, search the word, hear the word right, exhort one another and get actively involved in worshipping God, there is no enemy that can stand before us because it is the Lord's battle. And when it is fought God's way, the battle will get God's results.

2 Chron 20:22 And when they began to sing and to praise, the LORD set ambushments against the children of Ammon, Moab, and mount Seir, which were come against Judah; and they were smitten.

23 For the children of Ammon and Moab stood up against the inhabitants of mount Seir, utterly to slay and destroy them: and when they had made an end of the inhabitants of Seir, every one helped to destroy another. KJV

If you would notice; this was an unusual battle because the people of God did not use spears, knives, swords nor arrows; they simply relied on praising the name of the Lord. They did not wait to see what was going to happen; as they praised God the enemies turned on each other. This shows us how praise confuses the enemy, why he would like to see us silent, sad and dejected; he knows from experience that praise is a disturber to his camp.

Praising God is yet one of the most powerful weapons against the mightiest enemies; that is why Satan tries so hard to silence our voice when we are in the midst of trouble. Satan knows the powerful effect praise has upon his stuff; therefore, he tries to make things so miserable that we cannot offer praise.

Ps 50:23 Whoso offereth praise glorifieth me: and to him that ordereth his conversation aright will I shew the salvation of God. KJV

When we praise God right and talk right, the strongest, the largest, and the most severe problem in our lives must bow in the presence of our God. Just as Jehoshaphat and the children of Israel did not wait until the battle was over before they commenced to praise the Lord, neither should we because He said in His word that "Praise glorifies me." Therefore, He is worthy to be praised both in trouble and out; so let us get into the habit of praising Him regardless of the circumstances.

Ps 92:1 It is a good thing to give thanks unto the LORD, and to sing praises unto thy name, O most High: KJV

Trouble is a good time to know the Lord. But when we know Him in advance, we are protected from what the enemy has in mind. Furthermore, whatever the enemy does to us will work for our good because we love the Lord.

I am sure that the Hebrew boys didn't go into Babylon looking for trouble. However, they were well prepared for opposition because they had a real good relationship with the God of Heaven.

This is known to be true and so is it true that those who love the Lord are known to call upon Him in the time of trouble.

Ps 20:1The LORD hear thee in the day of trouble; the name of the God of Jacob defend thee; 2 Send thee help from the sanctuary, and strengthen thee out of Zion; KJV

The Hebrew boys were given a so-called choice; they could either bow to a manmade image or burn. The fact that their God was not made with hands had been ingrained into their spirits, so they had no fear of the enemy's fire. They knew God well enough to know that whatever trouble they were in, He would be in there with them. This is how the Lord would have us to know Him. Knowing Him the way the Hebrew boys knew Him will open doors for His greatness to be manifested and His glory to be seen by those who don't know Him. The poise of these three young men leaves no doubt they knew Him before the fire.

But, we need to be fireproofed before trouble ignites the flames. That is, we need to really know the Lord before a wave of affliction sweeps over our souls. It's good to acquaint ourselves with the Lord before the flames so that our focus is on Him rather than on what the enemy is doing. We cannot stop the devil from being an enemy and neither should we allow him to stop us from trusting our Lord.

We can see that the Hebrew boys were protected from the harm of the fire because they had a genuine relationship. A good relationship with the Lord is the believer's best fire protection plan. Making an application for this kind of fire protection on a daily basis serves to our advantage. You need to check the hidden clauses which offer deliverance either from or in sin, but for sure check their records for victories won and efforts defeated. For those who trust in Him will be delivered. Just because the enemy intensifies the heat to the seventh power, is no need to panic. The more difficult the enemy makes the problems the more the Lord is magnified.

Satan is greatly vexed when he sees his best efforts defeated. For that cause, he solicits all the support he can get. When he tried to destroy the Hebrew boys, he was able to get the assistance of the Babylonian authorities. However, the Hebrew boys had a greater backing because they were backed by the God of the heavenly host. One officer from heaven can do or undo more than tens of thousands of earth's creatures. Those of us who believe should thank God for His unwavering confidence that He displays in those who trust Him. We should be grateful for those that held fast under great trials. Those tested and tried soldiers that have proven over and over again that God not only can, but will deliver.

When we start believing that we are equipped to stand, we stand taller and we stand longer.

Eph 6:10 Finally, my brethren, be strong in the Lord, and in the power of his might.
11 Put on the whole armour of God, that ye may be able to stand against the wiles of the devil.

12 For we wrestle not against flesh and blood, but against principalities, against powers, against the rulers of the darkness of this world, against spiritual wickedness in high places.

13 Wherefore take unto you the whole armour of God, that ye may be able to withstand in the evil day, and having done all, to stand.

14 Stand therefore, having your loins girt about with truth, and having on the breastplate of righteousness;

15 And your feet shod with the preparation of the gospel of peace;

16 Above all, taking the shield of faith, wherewith ye shall be able to quench all the fiery darts of the wicked.

17 And take the helmet of salvation, and the sword of the Spirit, which is the word of God: KJV

Heb 6:18 That by two immutable things, in which it was impossible for God to lie, we might have a strong consolation, who have fled for refuge to lay hold upon the hope set before us: KJV

Titus 1:2 In hope of eternal life, which God, that cannot lie, promised before the world began; KJV

Num 23:19 God is not a man, that he should lie; neither the son of man, that he should repent: hath he said, and shall he not do it? or hath he spoken, and shall he not make it good? KJV

If your are a true believer, and are presently under attack, feed on God's word and your faith will rise to a level where you can see God work for you. Every time God does something for us it prepares us for the next situation. With every problem we encounter, we should seek to profit by seeking God's word on the situation. When we find God's word on it we will know that we are walking in the safety of God. Paul and Silas did not go to jail to get to know the Lord; that matter had been settled long before they were put in jail. No one can afford to wait until trouble attacks to ascertain his position in the Lord. This approach is faithless and is sure to prove the pressures of life too great to make a victory decision. It is always to our advantage to daily seek the face of God because we never know *when or how the enemy is going to show his troublemaking hand. It is not ours to decide what kind of test we want to come, and neither do we decide how long it is to stay; however, it is our responsibility to watch* and pray so that whatever comes we can maintain *fellowship with the Master.*

Paul and Silas evidently knew what the Word of God said about praising God at midnight.

Ps 119:62 At midnight I will rise to give thanks unto thee because of thy righteous judgments. KJV

Many think only of praising God at church or on special occasions, but here the man of God is suggesting the interruption of his sleep to send up praises. However, when we look at midnight as a time of trouble, trials or difficulty, then praising God would leave out the majority. Many people are made to feel that one should praise God when things are going well because midnight is not always a convenient time to praise the Lord.

For Paul and Silas, it may not have been convenient but they were willing to step out on the Word and do what was necessary. We all know from reading the text, that they did not only praise God in their hearts; but rather, they opened wide their mouths and offered praises unto the Lord, for the prisoners heard them. First they prayed; and when you pray right, it is no problem to praise right. Prayer will ignite the fire of praise and put wings on your spirit so that you can zoom into the presence of the Lord. Thank God, Paul and Silas did not wait until they got in jail to learn how to praise the Lord; they qualified themselves in the course of praising God long before the jail door clang shut upon them. I am sure that the Lord didn't leave the action of Paul and Silas on record just to make the book thicker, he wanted all that encounter life's difficulties to know that praise does more to set you free then complaining ever would. We should learn that circumstances don't have to be perfect to praise God, and that we need God in whatever we are in.

THE PRAISE EQUIPMENT

The source book for all praisers is the Bible; those who look into it will find plenty of support for praising the Almighty.

Ps 21:13 Be thou exalted, LORD, in thine own strength: so will we sing and praise thy power. KJV

When a believer praises God for His mighty power and many acts of kindness, he puts himself at God's disposal. It allows God to do what He does best which is to set the captive free.

When you think of praising the Lord, please remember that your mouth plays a vital part in praising Him. This is not to say that the mouth is the only part, or the only thing, that is used in praising the Lord. The Bible speaks about various instruments being used to praise Him. To truly benefit from this, we need to involve our total being in offering Him praise.

If you can recall, your mouth was open when you received the Holy Ghost, and many of us were saying words of praise. Now, if words of praise blessed us to get filled, what do you think would happen if we keep praising Him after being filled?

Praise is a command of action; therefore, there is no true praise without action. If you really want to upset the enemy, praise God with all of your might and strength. Better yet, offer a sacrifice of praise-that is, praise Him when you don't feel like it or when all odds are against you.

> *Heb 13:15 By him therefore let us offer the sacrifice of praise to God continually, that is, the fruit of our lips giving thanks to his name. KJV*

We seem to understand sacrifice until it comes to totally surrendering them to the Lord. We can easily give another dollar or some valuable gift, but when it comes to time, effort or involving ourselves in all-out praise to the Lord, then our understanding becomes deficient.

There was a time when the Apostolic Church was known for her style of worship-involved in the service, loud singing, and clapping, dancing, shouts of triumph with the voice. But today, we are quieter than some of the mainline groups. However, those who know the real meaning of praise did not just praise the Lord when it was popular and quit when the modern wave passed over; they are yet praising and shall continue to praise the Lord. When we familiarize ourselves with praising the Lord in the morning, we will have little trouble praising Him at midnight. Better yet, if we praise Him in the time of peace, He will inhabit our praise in the height of the battle.

> *Ps 34: I will bless the LORD at all times: his praise shall continually be in my mouth. KJV*

"All times" covers when we feel good, bad, and in between, sick, well, broke, disappointed, etc. Praising the Lord is therapeutic. The Bible has so much to say about the virtue and value of praise: "Let everything that hath breath praise the Lord." Ps 50:23

Whoso offereth praise glorifieth me: and to him that ordereth his conversation aright will I shew the salvation of God. KJV

God knows that we need that medicinal effect to help relieve us of our many pressures and to invite Him in to heal us where we hurt the most.

Just think what would have happened if Paul and Silas had sat there in jail complaining about how they were being mistreated, and that, after all, they were serving the Lord the best they knew how. "As much as we have done for the Lord, why would He let us get locked up in the first place?" If they had talked like that, we never would have read about the true "Jail House Rock." They would have disqualified themselves from "ordering their conversation aright"; they would have been speaking defeat and not victory; and talking bondage and not freedom. However, they ordered their conversation aright, and, in doing so, they glorified the Lord and He showed them His strong deliverance.

Now if you are suffering from a jail-like experience, you need to glorify Him in praise and watch Him show you His great salvation (deliverance). Paul and Silas, in their time of trouble, got involved in a good thing. They chose to do what was right, so they offered up praises unto the Lord and He brought them out. You can be sure that when one does his/her part, the Lord will always do His part, He tells us to offer praise and when we do, He makes Himself at home in the midst of praise.

> *Psalms 33:1 Rejoice in the LORD, O ye righteous: for praise is comely for the upright. KJV*

> *Ps 33:1 Let all the joys of the godly well up in praise to the Lord, for it is right to praise him. TLB*

> *Ps 92:1 It is a good thing to give thanks unto the LORD, and to sing praises unto thy name, O most High: KJV*

> *Ps 50:14 Offer unto God thanksgiving; and pay thy vows unto the most High:*

> *15 And call upon me in the day of trouble: I will deliver thee, and thou shalt glorify me. KJV*

When we say that we will bless the Lord, we should not allow anything to prevent us from offering unto the Lord what He rightfully deserves, this commitment should be in the light of whatever happens. If I understand what the Lord is saying, our deliverance is contingent upon our offering thanks. It is after we have offered thanks that we are then told to call upon Him. We want to call before we offer thanks, but let's do it right and give the Lord what he deserves the way He wants.

ENCOURAGING WORDS
IN A STORM

A storm has been defined as a violent outbreak or rage, or to advance an attack against something or someone. We learn from the Word of God that some storms come by name.

Acts 27:13 And when the south wind blew softly, supposing that they had obtained their purpose, loosing thence, they sailed close by Crete.

14 But not long after there arose against it a tempestuous wind, called Euroclydon. KJV

From all evidence, they thought it safe for them to travel because there was only a soft breeze blowing. But after they began to sail, they were met with a violent storm name Euroclydon. This storm is as typical as the storms of life, in as much as it seemed to have hit them unexpectedly, right when the sun was shining and the sailing was smooth. This is the typical pattern of life—hitting its victims unexpectedly. Those that know this are wise to prepare to the best of their ability while the sun is shinning. No doubt, trying to learn storm security measures during a storm could be hazardous. Likewise, trying to learn God during a storm could be costly.

The men aboard the ship did everything they could to make the ship safe, and that included throwing overboard everything they felt they could do without. This should be the mindset of every wise sailor on the sea of time, we should get rid of everything we can sail without: worry, stress, hatred, bitterness, envy, jealousy, hostility, criticism, anger, retaliation, and by all means get rid of every unforgiving spirit. These are things we can do without; in fact they are things that "so easily beset us" and make sailing more difficult, if not impossible.

When hit by a storm, only those things which are a part of our livelihood are important at that moment; everything else becomes excess baggage or rubbish. They threw out the tackling of the ship; in other words, they got rid of part of the ship's equipment. They were more concerned about survival than they were about how well-equipped the ship was.

When we are struck by one of life's storms, we should be careful to remove everything we think would make life more productive, or safe, for riding out the storm. I am convinced that we have held on to things during our storms that, without a doubt, would have been better cast out. The main objective in a storm should be to come out safe or better, or both.

Some storms are so violent that they take away all signs of safety and sometimes hope of survival. This was the kind of storm that hit the ship transporting Brother Paul.

Acts 27:20 And when neither sun nor stars in many days appeared, and no small tempest lay on us, all hope that we should be saved was then taken away. KJV

How often have you been hit by storms that take away the light by day and by night? These are the kinds of storms that make you thankful that you know the Lord. Because He is our light and our salvation, we do not have to fear when our darkness appear. He is there to see us through or to see to it that whatever happens will be for our good. Whenever a storm hits our life, it is to our advantage to be in a good relationship with the Lord, seeing how storms don't always warn us of their coming. Neither do they say how long they are going to stay, nor surely not how much damage are they going to do while they are there.

The states of Louisiana, Mississippi, Alabama and Florida, have just witnessed a storm called Katrina, she bore the name of a woman, but her blow was ever stronger than any woman or man. This storm was unpredictable from the beginning to the end. That is the way the storms of life are, that is why we need to know God in advance, we cannot wait until the storm strikes to make preparation we need to get busy seeking to know Him better everyday.

Sometimes storms bring such great darkness both by day and by night that it hides the sun and the moon and stars. But, we know the one who lights up our lives and His light will not be extinguished by life's storms.

Katrina left many in the dark. Many of us were unprepared for her visit. This is why she was so devastating in her rampage; however, our trust in the Lord prepares us for whatever storm comes our way. We may lose electrical power but we will never lose the light of the Son.

> *Ps 30:5 For his anger endureth but a moment; in his favour is life: weeping may endure for a night, but joy cometh in the morning. KJV*

All we have to do is endure the night because morning will bring joy. Because of this fact, Satan will do all he can to wipe us out during the night. He tries to make our nights so long and so dark that we lose all hope. He'd like to see us abandon the ship of Zion and return to our old lifestyle of looking for answers to our situation in all the wrong places while using the wrong practices. But all we need to do is hold out until the morning because joy is guaranteed.

Our best exercise during the night season, or the storms of life, is to tell ourselves that joy is coming in spite of the gloom. Morning is coming regardless of the darkness night; morning is coming! We must get that fact so embedded in our spirits that neither storm nor darkness nor anything else can blow it out of our spirit.

We are blessed when we are around someone who knows what's wrong how to get things right. Just knowing what is wrong will not always solve the problem; notwithstanding, it can help, and if it doesn't help, it sure won't hurt.

One of the greatest blessings to a person facing great odds is to know that everything is going to be all right. That is what God's word is about; it gives assurance to all believers that the Lord will not forsake His own. However, there may be times when it appears that He has gone, but He will never forsake us no matter what the problem or situation. The thing that made the ship safe was that God's man was on board to make God's word good for His servant; those who sailed with the servant of God were also protected.

The words spoken at the height of the storm were a reflection of Paul's relationship with the Lord. It was clear that Paul sensed the providential hand of God upon his life and the lives of those with him.

Acts 27:22 And now I exhort you to be of good cheer: for there shall be no loss of any man's life among you, but of the ship.

23 For there stood by me this night the angel of God, whose I am, and whom I serve,

24 Saying, Fear not, Paul; thou must be brought before Caesar: and, lo, God hath given thee all them that sail with thee.

25 Wherefore, sirs, be of good cheer: for I believe God, that it shall be even as it was told me. KJV

It is amazing to me how God always comes through when we need Him most and He knows exactly what to say in every given situation. God spoke hope to Paul when all hope seemed to have been gone; Paul relayed that hope to those with him. This should sound familiar to us because we have gone to the house of God many times during our personal storms and heard words of encouragement time and time again. God is known to show up either before or during each storm and then after every storm. He shows up beforehand to prepare us—to get us boarded up and sand bagged. He shows up during the storm to console us. He shows up afterwards to replenish us. (GLORY!!)

Neither does God have to move a mountain to make known His presence. All He has to do is speak a word in season to our troubled souls. Those who know Him recognize His voice—a voice that brings a peace that passeth all human understanding. (Remember I Kings 19:11,12? "The Lord passed by and a great and strong wind rent the mountains and brake in pieces the rock before the Lord, but the Lord was not in the wind: and after the wind, an earthquake, but the Lord was not in the earthquake: and after the earthquake a fire; but the Lord was not in the fire: and after the fire a still small voice.")

Faith-filled words in troublesome times are like sunshine after a rain or a breath of fresh air in a stifling place. The men aboard the ship were, no doubt, troubled about the severity of the storm and about the loss they had already suffered. However, they were blessed to have a true man of God on board, one that was truly in touch with the master over every situation.

It is a great advantage to be in the presence of a person that is in touch with the Lord. Heretofore already declared, while attending the house of God, we should come with the spirit of expectation because God's servant has stood in the presence of God and stands ready, willing and able to encourage the lives of God's children that are wrestling in a storm.

Because the Lord is so mindful of us, He always sends us a word in season to fortify our position in the time of trouble. Every storm that comes upon us is carefully watched by His all seeing eyes; He will not let a wind, rain, blizzard or anything else fall upon us that exceeds our ability to stand. This is comforting to know that God weighs every test, trial, burden, problem and every measure of opposition before it is allowed to come upon us. Knowing this should help us stand even the more because we know that God is aware of what we are dealing with and that He knows also that we are equipped to stand.

It is very common for the Lord to send us a word of encouragement before the storm so that we can be well prepared to stand. However, if we do not receive our word *before* the storm, we must not let the rage of the storm drown His voice because He is sure to speak *during* the storm. Just as God visited Paul and assured him that everything was going to be all right, He, likewise, will visit you, and give His own personal weather report, His report says that everything is going to be all right.

Without a doubt, we would all perish in the midst of the sea of trouble if it wasn't for that heavenly visitation that comes our way so often. It is not uncommon for the Christian to go from one storm to another. For those who are living for the True and Living God in this hostile world, righteous living is enough of an invitation for the contrary winds to keep blowing upon us. However, we need not fear because the Lord knows what He has put in us and the devil is trying to find out the secret.

Just as Satan is good at sending storms, the Lord is even better at calming the storms that the devil sends. So be encouraged, you are near the shores of safety and the Lord Himself is the captain of every believer's ship. But, to remain safe, you must stay on board regardless of how the winds blow or the waves splash; just cleave to the fact that Jesus is there to see you through.

Satan loves to make the picture much darker than it really is; he hopes to provoke us to abandon the safety of God. That is why encouragement is so precious to the souls of all believers. God's word is a lamp unto our feet; therefore, we can see where we are through the word. We do not have to walk in darkness or stumble at noon because He lights our path through His word.

The final verse of Acts 27 concludes that they all made it to the shore safely; God confirmed His word that He spoke during the storm. God said that none would be lost. He does not have to wait to see what is going to happen before He speaks because He knows the end from the beginning and all points between.

Rom 4:17(As it is written, I have made thee a father of many nations,) before him whom he believed, even God, who quickeneth the dead, and calleth those things which be not as though they were. KJV

In other words, God does not have to wait and see it in order to say it because He is a "faith God" or a God of faith. He wants us to be people of faith because faith is given to walk by and to live by.

Gal 3:11 But that no man is justified by the law in the sight of God, it is evident: for, The just shall live by faith. KJV Hab 2:4 Behold, his soul which is lifted up is not upright in him: but the just shall live by his faith. KJV

Rom 1:17 For therein is the righteousness of God revealed from faith to faith: as it is written, The just shall live by faith. KJV

Heb 10:39 But we are not of them who draw back unto perdition; but of them that believe to the saving of the soul. KJV

We can clearly see that faith is the thing that the just lives by. Whatever we seek from the Lord is obtained by faith. Anything that faith can't order, I would like to think that we do not need it, and surely couldn't enjoy it because it would be strange to our spiritual nature. We are a people of faith, saved by faith, kept by faith, walk by faith, and stand by faith and serve the Lord by faith. We expect Him to come and receive us unto Himself by faith.

Mark 11:22 And Jesus answering saith unto them, Have faith in God.

23 For verily I say unto you, That whosoever shall say unto this mountain, Be thou removed, and be thou cast into the sea; and shall not doubt in his heart, but shall believe that those things which he saith shall come to pass; he shall have whatsoever he saith.

24 Therefore I say unto you, What things soever ye desire, when ye pray, believe that ye receive them, and ye shall have them. KJV

It is impossible to please God without faith; we must believe Him in order to come to Him. We must believe Him in order to follow Him because the road that He travels is a dangerous road and we must believe that He is with us and that He will see us safely through.

Heb 11:6 But without faith it is impossible to please him: for he that cometh to God must believe that he is, and that he is a rewarder of them that diligently seek him. KJV

Therefore, we are to understand that our problems are viewed properly by faith. We are not obligated to see our way; we just need to believe that the Lord knows the way that we take. Our "child like" dependence on the Lord places us in the arena of faith. Whenever we stand in the arena of faith, we are made more than conquerors because the Lord is our refuge and strength. All the Lord ever needs is someone to stand on His promises; He is committed to do the rest.

We can see that the ship was demolished by the storm, but every soul of them arrived to shore safely. Some were said to have arrived safely on pieces of the ship; nevertheless, they all arrived alive. They had a promise that no lives would be lost, they were not promised that they would arrive in style; God's word was fulfilled in the fact that no lives were lost.

We should shout praises unto the Lord because He is never intimidated by life's storms no matter how severe they are. You can be sure that Satan will intensify every storm with hopes of blowing us out of the water. When we are anchored in Jesus, we may lose the ship, but we are sure to arrive safely on the other shore.

I think of the many ideas people have expressed through the years of how they feel that heaven will be. Some have said that they would walk all around God's heaven while others say that they are going to tell Jesus how they were treated while traveling along life's highway, and the list goes on and on. I doubt if any of the foregone ideas are of any importance. There is one thing I know is important, and that is arriving safely to that city. This is what we are promised by the Lord—that we can be where He is. The things we encounter between here and heaven should be insignificant in comparison to the desire of getting to that city called heaven. What someone did to us or did not do for us will not matter when we see the all encompassing face of Jesus.

No, indeed, we do not go out looking for storms. However, if we keep living right the storms will come. Satan will not sit idly by and watch us freely do what he did at one time-that is worship the Lord. Worshipping the Lord will enrage Satan's jealousy and he will try to stop, divert, or pollute our praise and worship. If he fails in his attempt, he will try to make life so miserable that it would be humanly impossible to enjoy our salvation, and heartfelt worship would be completely out of the question. Satan will send storm after storm in hopes of turning us from the Lord instead of us running to Him. But, the Lord has a word for us in times like these; we just need to lay hold on it and see the salvation of the Lord. As we read in the Word of God, we see time after time the Lord sending His word to fortify the hearts of His people in times of storms.

Ex 14:13 And Moses said unto the people, Fear ye not, stand still, and see the salvation of the LORD, which he will shew to you to day: for the Egyptians whom ye have seen to day, ye shall see them again no more for ever.

14 The LORD shall fight for you, and ye shall hold your peace. KJV

Deut 1:29 Then I said unto you, Dread not, neither be afraid of them.

30 The LORD your God which goeth before you, he shall fight for you, according to all that he did for you in Egypt before your eyes;

31 And in the wilderness, where thou hast seen how that the LORD thy God bare thee, as a man doth bear his son, in all the way that ye went, until ye came into this place. KJV

Deut 20:1 When thou goest out to battle against thine enemies, and seest horses, and chariots, and a people more than thou, be not afraid of them: for the LORD thy God is with thee, which brought thee up out of the land of Egypt. KJV

Deut 20:4 For the LORD your God is he that goeth with you, to fight for you against your enemies, to save you. KJV

Deut 31:6 Be strong and of a good courage, fear not, nor be afraid of them: for the LORD thy God, he it is that doth go with thee; he will not fail thee, nor forsake thee. KJV

2 Chron 32:7 Be strong and courageous, be not afraid nor dismayed for the king of Assyria, nor for all the multitude that is with him: for there be more with us than with him:

8 With him is an arm of flesh; but with us is the LORD our God to help us, and to fight our battles. And the people rested themselves upon the words of Hezekiah king of Judah. KJV

These Scriptures are just a few examples of how our God addresses His people in times of crises. Once we get His word we have what it takes to be encouraged in our situations?

One may say that the preceding Scriptures are from the Old Testament. This is true, but our God is in both Testaments. Let us see how He talks in the New Testament to those that are facing life's difficulties.

Phil 4: 6 Don't worry about anything; instead, pray about everything; tell God your needs, and don't forget to thank him for his answers.

7 If you do this, you will experience God's peace, which is far more wonderful than the human mind can understand. His peace will keep your thoughts and your hearts quiet and at rest as you trust in Christ Jesus. TLB

Grasping these words, brings us to see that the storm was a blessing to us because the storm made it necessary for us to experience these wonderful, peaceful and comforting words.

It is amazing to me how Satan keeps sending his storms into our lives only to have them diverted by God's loving word. There is not, nor will be, a storm that blows upon our lives that God's word has not already addressed; however, it is our responsibility to find that word, and rest upon its promise.

Ps 119:92 Unless thy law had been my delight I should then have perished in mine affliction. KJV

Ps 119:71 It is good for me that I have been afflicted; that I might learn thy statutes. KJV

Satan tries to blow us out of the water so to speak, but he ends up blowing us into a greater knowledge of God than we could ever imagine because we go to the Word of God for answers. When we are not clear on the word we receive from the Lord, we go to the house of the Lord and there the servant of the Lord sheds more light on the word and we leave God's house illuminated and strengthened. The next time you are in a storm, don't look at its severity or size; rather, look for Jesus because He is known to calm the raging sea with His Word. Therefore, anytime you get His word activated in you spirit, you have the Master on board and the storm cannot destroy you, it can only work for your good.

Storms are a necessary part of the Christian life because they help develop our character as well as blow the unnecessary dross out of our lives. No, we are not always joyful when the winds are raging, but when it is all over we are left better and stronger in our relationship with the Lord, and we are still standing. For that cause, we are able to view the storms differently.

Storms are necessary to help us see how safe we are in the hands of God. After we have been hit, but yet left standing, our confidence level is raised to a higher degree. We move from "I heard He could" to "I know He can and will do it for me."

Those who weather the storms of life find a place in God called the secret place; in that place, we might be hit, but the blows are not as severe as they would be if we were not abiding under the shadow of the Almighty.

IF YOU ARE SOLD OUT, YOU CAN HOLD OUT

When a person begins his or her walk with the Lord, holding out is one of his or her main concerns. There is always that question, "Will I be able to hold out?" All of us come to the Lord knowing more about losing than we know about winning. That's because we came from Satan's kingdom where there are nothing but losers. It wasn't until we entered into God's kingdom that we we discovered that there is a real devil and that he is the enemy of God seeking to turn around any and everybody that tries to make heaven their home. Satan isn't choosy as to how he turns aside a believing soul, just as long as he gets the job done. Since Satan is not everywhere at the same time, he depends on his agents to help him in his attempt to turn souls away from the kingdom. He will also solicit help from any human, Christian or non-Christian is no real concern just as long as he stops men from serving the Lord. Our success in holding out is more than human effort, it is a divine plan. God knew before He called us that He was able to keep whatever is committed unto Him. Therefore, to hold out, we should start by committing our total being to His care and abiding in His Word.

It is a scriptural fact that the people that accomplished the most for the Lord were those that counted not their own lives dear, but put the Lord's calling first and foremost. People that are sold out choose to do so because their desire is to please the Lord by following Him faithfully to the end. Sold out people are not crowd pleasers, nor do they seek man's approval; their commitment is to Christ alone. They know that if Jesus can't do it, it just cannot be done. And when others leave the assignment, they seem to become more determined.

> *John 6:66 From that time many of his disciples went back, and walked no more with him.*
>
> *67 Then said Jesus unto the twelve, Will ye also go away?*
>
> *68 Then Simon Peter answered him, Lord, to whom shall we go? thou hast the words of eternal life.*
>
> *69 And we believe and are sure that thou art that Christ, the Son of the living God. KJV*

When you are sold out, public opinions are secondary because Christ is everything to you (that is, when you are really committed). To those that are committed, it is no real problem to overcome prestige, power, riches or popularity. It was this kind of commitment that enabled Moses to make his big decision in regards to forsaking Egypt.

> *Heb 11:24 By faith Moses, when he was come to years, refused to be called the son of Pharaoh's daughter;*
>
> *25 Choosing rather to suffer affliction with the people of God, than to enjoy the pleasures of sin for a season;*
>
> *26 Esteeming the reproach of Christ greater riches than the treasures in Egypt: for he had respect unto the recompence of the reward. KJV*

Summing up Moses' decision, we have to conclude that he gave up a fortune for a future. This is the kind of vision found in those who are sold out; they are also the ones that will hold out. We must at all times remember that the world will do all it can to hold us in its grip, hoping to smother our desire for the Lord. But when we are sold out, we can hold out. If we wait for opposition to arise before we decide on being sold out, trouble, trials and circumstances will drown us.

Today's Christians of other denominations are guilty of looking upon the biblical saints as professing to be holier, better, or maybe even closer to God than we really are. The difference I see in us and them is in the realm of commitment. The saints of old seemingly took their relationship as a matter of life and death. It could be said of them that they would rather die for Christ than to dance with the world. This is not to say that Christians today don't possess the same feelings, it's just that the numbers that do are in such small quantity. I must admit, there was a time in my day that the pledge of a Christian meant more than it does today. There was a time when if you got a Christian's word on a thing, you could bank on it, but now you had better wait and see.

We cannot blame our loss of dedication on the devil because it isn't that he has become worse. That's an impossibility; he's already the epitome of evil—been that all the time. The deficiency is in us. We have just stopped doing what we know to do to keep him in his place. No, the devil is no worse now than he was the first day he appeared in human affairs; however, our defense has relaxed. We can credit our love for ease, comfort and the desire to be accepted by the world as the main reasons why we are not as dedicated as we used to be. Some do not fare better in walking with the Lord because they fail to commit their lives to the Lord first of all, and then many fail to realize that they are taking on the entire system of the world. Satan is the god of this world, and his system will support his efforts by doing whatever is necessary to keep saints from making it over to the safe side of life. Those who fall in love with the world, or compromise with it, stand very little chance of survival under his management. However, those true soldiers that are sold out know that they are not home yet and that the fight they are in is a good fight. They know that to stay close to Jesus is to win every round. The quote that best describes a real soldier of the cross is: "When the going gets tough, the tough gets going." The main preparation for God's marching army is found in the Word of God. In God's Word believers can find plenty of support for doing what we are doing. Examples abound of the reward of holding out until God works things out. Anytime we get the feeling that we are home, or get to feeling too comfortable in this system, the Apostle John will talk to us:

1 John 2:15 Love not the world, neither the things that are in the world. If any man love the world, the love of the Father is not in him.

16 For all that is in the world, the lust of the flesh, and the lust of the eyes, and the pride of life, is not of the Father, but is of the world.

17 And the world passeth away, and the lust thereof: but he that doeth the will of God abideth for ever. KJV

If the world tries to stain us with its system of lust and greed, Peter will speak to us:

1 Peter 2:11 Dearly beloved, I beseech you as strangers and pilgrims, abstain from fleshly lusts, which war against the soul; KJV

Every conscientious person should strive to keep his soul out of jeopardy. When the world attacks with lust and pride, we can be sure that Satan is trying to make us feel at home. Satan would like for us to become intoxicated with this world's system and stay drunk long enough to miss out on the next trip to heaven. However, Jesus Himself warned us to watch out for this old trick.

Luke 21:34 And take heed to yourselves, lest at any time your hearts be overcharged with surfeiting, and drunkenness, and cares of this life, and so that day come upon you unawares. KJV

Our fight is not centered on just one enemy, but rather, one enemy with many avenues to launch his approach. Our best and only real defense is our love and devotion to our Lord and Savior, Jesus Christ. Loving Jesus will inspire us to pledge our lives to Him. This is what gave the saints of old over-whelming success, their love, devotion and vision of spending eternity with Jesus. Whenever the thought of spending eternity with Jesus grips the heart, the charm of this life loses its glamour. Nothing appeals to us like entering into His presence, to never depart. I tell you, this is worth fighting for.

When we think of Abraham, Joseph, Moses and many others, we can see something other than toughness; we can see that they had a devout relationship with the Lord. It was that wholehearted devotion that fortified them in times of great difficulties; they remained focused and committed to the Lord.

The same principles which successfully safeguarded men of old are the same rules all men are to abide by. If we walk by the same rules, we get the same results. As Christians, we must keep in mind that just because one is sold out to Jesus, they are by no means removed from trouble. Just the opposite is closer to the truth. We cannot, therefore, look upon our new relationship with Jesus as having escaped to the land of freedom without opposition. Rather, we are called to the war zone where the battle is in the heat of the day. Notwithstanding, through faith, we know who will win. We are in the Lord's army; our Lord has never lost a battle and is sure to win the one we are in at the present. Since Christ cannot lose, that makes those who abide in Him more than conquerors.

It is good that we have the Bible to enlighten us on the outcome of our future as well as the many encounters we will face because. According to the Word, believers are winners in the end. The Bible assures us that whatever happens to us will work for good as long as we love the Lord and are "the called."

Rom 8:28 And we know that all things work together for good to them that love God, to them who are the called according to his purpose. KJV

1 Peter 4:1 Forasmuch then as Christ hath suffered for us in the flesh, arm yourselves likewise with the same mind: for he that hath suffered in the flesh hath ceased from sin; KJV

When we know what to expect, we can better prepare ourselves for whatever the enemy brings against us. The better prepared we are, the less damage is done to our minds, souls and spirits through the attacks of the enemy. While we are not in a position to say what should happen to us, we are in a position to say what we are going to do about what happens to us. That is to say, we are going to cleave more closely to the Lord regardless of what happens. We will not let anything come between us and our relationship with the Lord. This is the only attitude we can afford; anything less would place us at the enemy's disposal to do with us as he pleases.

Our position is greatly strengthened when we look into the Word of God and see how those, who were committed, fared. This knowledge should elevate us to the level of thinking that if anyone else can, so can we; and if bad things happened to other good people, why not me? The Word of God tells us where to look in our struggles because good examples are a necessary part of our walk with Him. They help to keep us focused and encouraged.

Heb 12:2 Keep your eyes on Jesus, our leader and instructor. He was willing to die a shameful death on the cross because of the joy he knew would be his afterwards; and now he sits in the place of honor by the throne of God.

3 If you want to keep from becoming faint-hearted and weary, think about his patience as sinful men did such terrible things to him. 4 After all, you have never yet struggled against sin and temptation until you sweat great drops of blood. TLB

Jesus is our supreme example because no one suffered like He did; neither has anyone demonstrated patience like He did in His sufferings. It is one thing to suffer and yet another to bear it without complaining or trying to squirm out of it. Jesus suffered for us, leaving us an example to follow.

1 Peter 2:21 For even hereunto were ye called: because Christ also suffered for us, leaving us an example, that ye should follow his steps: KJV

Whenever we are tempted to complain or to become weary, we can focus on Jesus and draw strength to endure. We understand that through Jesus Christ the cross precedes the crown, typifying the truth that those who forfeit the cross will nullify the crown. Those who are spiritually deep, and cannot associate the sufferings of Jesus with our sufferings can draw from the many human examples that are listed in the 11ᵗʰ chapter of Hebrews.

Heb 11:33 Who through faith subdued kingdoms, wrought righteousness, obtained promises, stopped the mouths of lions,

34 Quenched the violence of fire, escaped the edge of the sword, out of weakness were made strong, waxed valiant in fight, turned to flight the armies of the aliens.

35 Women received their dead raised to life again: and others were tortured, not accepting deliverance; that they might obtain a better resurrection:

36 And others had trial of cruel mockings and scourgings, yea, moreover of bonds and imprisonment:

37 They were stoned, they were sawn asunder, were tempted, were slain with the sword: they wandered about in sheepskins and goatskins; being destitute, afflicted, tormented;

38 (Of whom the world was not worthy:) they wandered in deserts, and in mountains, and in dens and caves of the earth.

39 And these all, having obtained a good report through faith, received not the promise:

40 God having provided some better thing for us, that they without us should not be made perfect. KJV

The saints mentioned above were totally committed to Christ; "they loved not their lives unto the death." They believed that death could only place them in His presence forever. When we live with this kind of assurance, life has more to offer, and tragedies are seen as stepping stones or triumphs. As much as we dislike trouble and trials, when we are totally committed to God, the blows are not nearly as damaging as they would be or as they are to those that are not committed. The non-committed run to whatever they think will relieve their present pressures. This will vary depending on the spiritual status of the individual. And if they are just going through the motions, they will turn to drinking, smoking, doping, cursing, gambling, and rambling and whatever else they think will bring them quick relief. But the righteous will find refuge under the shadow of the Almighty, who is our shelter in the time of storm.

Ps 91:1 He that dwelleth in the secret place of the most High shall abide under the shadow of the Almighty.

*2 I will say of the LORD, He is my refuge
and my fortress: my God; in him will I trust.
KJV*

"For me to write the same thing for me indeed
is not grievous." The whole objective of this Holy
Spirit inspired writing is to saturate the seat of your
intellect with this truth:

**Having the Lord as our refuge does not
prevent difficulties from coming. This just guarantees that we are safe in His care. Knowing this
will soften the blows and keep us from being** over-
thrown by doubt and fear when God allows a storm
to come through. Believers have never claimed to be
untouchable; we are just told that abiding under the
shadow of the Almighty is our protection. So, while
the storms of life are raging, we must keep abiding
and the Lord promises to keep right on blessing us
over and over again.

God not only visits us through the preached and
taught word, He also visits us in our daily devotion of
prayer and Scripture reading. Out of these methods,
we are qualified to encourage ourselves from time
to time. Speaking God's promises is a blessing to
us any time our ears hear what God's word has said
from our mouth. It is good for our ears to hear the
Word of God.

*Rom 10:17 So then faith cometh by hearing,
and hearing by the word of God. KJV*

Nothing encourages and fortifies us like hearing the Word of God. The Word is living and active and brings life into the spirit of those who give heed to it. Supernatural things happen when we hear the Word of God; our spirits are inflamed with spiritual insight and wisdom. God's word brings change into our spiritual condition like nothing else can or will, it also brings conviction and conversion.

Ps 19:7 The law of the LORD is perfect, converting the soul: the testimony of the LORD is ure, making wise the simple.

8 The statutes of the LORD are right, rejoicing the heart: the commandment of the LORD is pure, enlightening the eyes.

9 The fear of the LORD is clean, enduring for ever: the judgments of the LORD are true and righteous altogether.

10 More to be desired are they than gold, yea, than much fine gold: sweeter also than honey and the honeycomb.

11 Moreover by them is thy servant warned: and in keeping of them there is great reward. KJV

YOU WILL NEVER WALK ALONE

One of the things that concerns and challenges us most in life is the thought of being alone. The more we face things that we cannot handle, the more we crave for someone or something to lean on. Even the man living in sin will seek for help in the times of trouble. However, the children of God have His word that He will never leave us nor forsake us. It is this kind of assurance that makes the twenty-third Psalms so beautiful; the writer could see God as an ever abiding presence.

Ps 23 The LORD is my shepherd; I shall not want.

2 He maketh me to lie down in green pastures: he leadeth me beside the still waters.

3 He restoreth my soul: he leadeth me in the paths of righteousness for his name's sake.

4 Yea, though I walk through the valley of the shadow of death, I will fear no evil: for thou art with me; thy rod and thy staff they comfort me.

5 Thou preparest a table before me in the presence of mine enemies: thou anointest my head with oil; my cup runneth over.

6 Surely goodness and mercy shall follow me all the days of my life: and I will dwell in the house of the LORD for ever. KJV

David could see that by having the Lord abiding with him, nothing but good could happen to him. This is, no doubt, the vision that the Apostle Paul had in the Eighth Chapter of Romans that caused him to ask his age-old question about being separated from God's love.

Rom 8:35 Who shall separate us from the love of Christ? shall tribulation, or distress, or persecution, or famine, or nakedness, or peril, or sword?

36 As it is written, For thy sake we are killed all the day long; we are accounted as sheep for the slaughter.

37 Nay, in all these things we are more than conquerors through him that loved us.

38 For I am persuaded, that neither death, nor life, nor angels, nor principalities, nor powers, nor things present, nor things to come,

39 Nor height, nor depth, nor any other creature, shall be able to separate us from the love of God, which is in Christ Jesus our Lord. KJV

Ps 3:6 I will not be afraid of ten thousands of people, that have set themselves against me round about. KJV

Ps 27:3 Though an host should encamp against me, my heart shall not fear: though war should rise against me, in this will I be confident. KJV

Ps 118:6 The LORD is on my side; I will not fear: what can man do unto me? KJV
Prov 3:24 When thou liest down, thou shalt not be afraid: yea, thou shalt lie down, and thy sleep shall be sweet. KJV

Isa 12:2 Behold, God is my salvation; I will trust, and not be afraid: for the LORD JEHOVAH is my strength and my song; he also is become my salvation. KJV

If any one thing is clear in the Scriptures, it is the fact that we do not travel alone because the Lord is with those who put their trust in Him. Our faith is increased in the Lord by the things He does because we know that He is no respecter of persons and all who trust Him experience His protection. Furthermore, He gives us His word so that we might know what equipment belongs to us and its proper use.

Rom 15:4 For whatsoever things were written aforetime were written for our learning, that we through patience and comfort of the scriptures might have hope. KJV

When we start searching the Word of God and see how miraculously the hand of God was upon those who trusted His salvation, our faith increases. God's word is living; therefore, when we read what He did, it puts life in our spirit and faith in our hearts. The more we hear it, the more we desire to see Him do the same for us.

In every situation we face, we can look to the Word of God for comfort, encouragement, guidance, courage and strength. The Lord knows where we are, and He knows what we need to help us endure. It can never be said in truth that the Lord abandons His trusting followers. Even if we seem alone, His Spirit is very present; if the night offers no light and the sunshine refuses to come through, He is there watching our development and securing our safety.

There is no need for the Lord to get in a hurry because it is impossible for Him to be late. It is a fact that He is an "on time God." Now, there are times when He appears to be late, but that is only from the human view point, due to our own short patience.

We have grown accustomed to having what we want when we want it. However, God's timing and our timing are not on the same wave length. For us, a brief period of suffering is a long time. The Lord brings deliverance after we have suffered a little while; and our "little whiles" are not the same.

1 Peter 5:10 After you have suffered a little while, our God, who is full of kindness through Christ, will give you his eternal glory. He personally will come and pick you up, and set you firmly in place, and make you stronger than ever. TLB

It will bless us in the fire to remember that the Lord is watching the temperature and He knows when we have been in long enough. The reason He doesn't prematurely deliver us is that He wants us to come out stronger and better than we were before we went in. just knowing that He is there should be comfort enough because His record of delivering on time is undisputed. When He does not deliver us from the fire, He gets into situations with us to make sure we come out unharmed. This is what He did for the Hebrew boys.

Dan 3:24 Then Nebuchadnezzar the king was astonied, and rose up in haste, and spake, and said unto his counsellers, Did not we cast three men bound into the midst of the fire? They answered and said unto the king, True, O king.

25 He answered and said, Lo, I see four men loose, walking in the midst of the fire, and they have no hurt; and the form of the fourth is like the Son of God. KJV

The next day, the children of God were seen walking around in the fire unharmed and accompanied with a supernatural guest. It doesn't matter where we are, the Lord is known to be with us; all we have to do is just stay with Him. This is not to say that staying with the Lord eliminates all our problems. More than likely our increased devotion creates more problems. But one thing is for sure, we will never have to worry about the Lord forsaking us. There has never been a battle so heated or a storm so severe or night so dark that the Lord's presence has abandoned those who believe in Him. He was God in the flood; He was God at the Red Sea; at the Cliff Ziz. He was God in the face of the giant; in the fire; in the lions' den and anywhere else Satan chose to show his hand. Each time the enemy showed up and showed out, the Lord made known His mighty presence in due time. He took what the enemy attempted to do and converted it into a blessing for His believing children.

We can be sure that time has not made Him any less concerned over the welfare of His children; He is yet our shepherd, and our ever abiding companion. We don't have to set the battle in motion when we choose to walk with the Lord; our assignment is to faithfully prepare to STAND before whatever comes. We know before it's over that we have been given the victory through our Lord and Savior Jesus Christ.

If we spent time developing our relationship with the One who called us to be soldiers, even our Lord and Savior Jesus Christ, we shall be more confident when we are under attack. It is the Lord's battle as much as the sheep's defense is the shepherd's duty. Have you ever seen or heard of fighting sheep? To my knowledge, they do not bleat nor run away. They just STAND. Since we are the sheep of His pasture, it behooves us to practice the behavior of sheep and learn to stay out of our Shepherd's way as He fights on our behalf.

Lately, we have heard much about the power of the universal 911 and its efficient accessibility to the aid of the citizens in its area. However, God has always had an emergency number for His children, not limited to any particular geographical nor spiritual area. It is effective for all men everywhere, especially to the righteous. According to Psalm 91 (and countless other passages) the righteous is always under divine surveillance, and nothing can befall them without the Lord's knowledge. He sees every change, good or other wise, in the Senate Chambers or on Wall Street, and He knows when we need His help. Isaiah 65:23-24 promises the seed of the blessed that He will answer before they call and while they are yet speaking He will hear. He patiently waits for us to make the right call, and when we call, we are guaranteed that our cry is heard and will be answered.

Ps 34:15 The eyes of the LORD are upon the righteous, and his ears are open unto their cry. KJV Ps 121:4 Behold, he that keepeth Israel shall neither slumber nor sleep. KJV

The fact that the Lord is awake at all times assures us that we can lie down and sleep since the watchful eyes of the Lord are upon us and His ears are awaiting our call. If we allow our problems to dominate our thinking, we lose much sleep and will be less effective than if we put our trust in the Lord and rest upon His word. He will give us sleep and rest!

Ps 4:8 I will both lay me down in peace, and sleep: for thou, LORD, only makest me dwell in safety. KJV

Ps 127:2 It is vain for you to rise up early, to sit up late, to eat the bread of sorrows: for so he giveth his beloved sleep. KJV

Sleep is a gift from God which He gives to His children to revive our bodies for the next day's labor. If we let worry and anxiety rob us of this gift, we will be guilty of shortening our lives and lessening our ability to perform our mission. Therefore, the next time you are troubled to the point you lose your sleep, get God's word on the matter; read it aloud and rehearse it over and over until it gets in your spirit, them praise God and go to bed and go to sleep.

Prov 3:24 When thou liest down, thou shalt not be afraid: yea, thou shalt lie down, and thy sleep shall be sweet. KJV

Again I say, our relationship with the Lord plays a very important role in our ability to deal with life's problems. When we stand firm in His word, we are able to draw His strength; and when we draw His strength, we are invincible in the face of the enemy. Instead of being controlled by fear, anxiety and worry, let us devote our energy to loving the Lord and abiding in His word because the rest is up to Him.

Prov 4:20 My son, attend to my words; incline thine ear unto my sayings.

21 Let them not depart from thine eyes; keep them in the midst of thine heart.

22 For they are life unto those that find them, and health to all their flesh. KJV
The believer's "watch word" is not just look out for the devil, but to attend unto the Word of God and keep it before our eyes, and it will do the rest. It is the Word that begets us and it takes the Word to keep us.

Ps 119:11 Thy word have I hid in mine heart, that I might not sin against thee. KJV

James 1:21 Wherefore lay apart all filthiness and superfluity of naughtiness, and receive with meekness the engrafted word, which is able to save your souls. KJV

Heb 4:12 For the word of God is quick, and powerful, and sharper than any twoedged sword, piercing even to the dividing asunder of soul and spirit, and of the joints and marrow, and is a discerner of the thoughts and intents of the heart. KJV

Thank God for the surgical ability of His Word which has the sharpness to reach the very core of our needs and the proficiency to remove and/or implant whatever is needed. The Word is effective in the body, mind and spirit; it serves us in life and will raise us in death.

For the children of the living God, there is only one call we need to frequent: calling upon the name of the Lord. We can be sure that if we keep calling, He will keep hearing and answering. Our God respects importunity.

Ps 34:6 This poor man cried, and the LORD heard him, and saved him out of all his troubles. KJV

Ps 120:1In my distress I cried unto the LORD, and he heard me. KJV

Being under attack is not the only time we should call upon the Lord. However, it is the most rewarding time to know that we can call upon Him, to experience His deliverance, and to rejoice in His merciful faithfulness. He will answer!! When we put our full trust in Him, He takes full responsibility in delivering us from our troubles.

> *Ps 34:17 The righteous cry, and the LORD heareth, and delivereth them out of all their troubles. KJV*

He didn't say that He would deliver us out of some of our troubles. He promised out of all of our troubles. Knowing this should stimulate our love for His presence even the more because He is always mindful of us, even when our thoughts are not directed toward Him. He is willing to share each burden and to answer every need in our life. He makes us safe on every side and assures us that deliverance will come in every affliction.

> *Ps 34:19 Many are the afflictions of the righteous: but the LORD delivereth him out of them all. KJV*

This is good news to the righteous and bad news for the enemy because Satan knows that God will keep His word; and when He says "all," God really means all. Just because Satan increases the heat, by no means signal God's bailing out and leaving us to perish. It only means that the increased heat of the enemy sets the stage for a mighty deliverance by the Mighty God who is well able to take over the production of the play and deliver us out of all our afflictions.

Jude 24 Now unto him that is able to keep you from falling, and to present you fault- less before the presence of his glory with exceeding joy, KJV

When the Lord brings us out, it gives us cause for rejoicing with exceeding joy because the Lord has done it again. We have all the reasons in the world to be confident because the Lord has so plainly set forth in His word His protection plan for the righteous. It is not a one way situation where everything is left on our shoulders; but to the contrary, we are under His watchful care every second. Just because He doesn't always come the moment we think He should, does not mean that He is not coming in His own time. God has a history of being on time for every call or to meet every need. He is concerned about us devel- oping His character, and that takes time and testing. When we are going through those periods of testing or discipline, we are being taught something that we cannot learn any other way.

Heb 12:9 Since we respect our fathers here on earth, though they punish us, should we not all the more cheerfully submit to God's training so that we can begin really to live?

10 Our earthly fathers trained us for a few brief years, doing the best for us that they knew how, but God's correction is always right and for our best good, that we may share his holiness. 11 Being punished isn't enjoyable while it is happening-it hurts! But afterwards we can see the result, a quiet growth in grace and character. TLB

It is the end result of suffering that the Lord favors for the life of His children because of the development that suffering brings into our lives. Furthermore, we have His word that He will be with us and that He will deliver us. We also have His guarantee that we will be made better after we have passed the test.

1 Peter 5:10 After you have suffered a little while, our God, who is full of kindness through Christ, will give you his eternal glory. He personally will come and pick you up, and set you firmly in place, and make you stronger than ever. TLB

In order for us to have more character, we need more testing. To be a better you and me, we need the important instruments of troubles and trials for our development.

Rom 5:3 And not only so, but we glory in tribulations also: knowing that tribulation worketh patience;

4 And patience, experience; and experience, hope:

5 And hope maketh not ashamed; because the love of God is shed abroad in our hearts by the Holy Ghost which is given unto us. KJV

God is our perfect example of suffering, and since His plan is well put together, when things go His way we are made more like Him.

"For this is thankworthy, if a man for conscience toward God endure grief, suffering wrongfully.

20 For what glory is it, if, when ye be buffeted for your faults, ye shall take it patiently? but if, when ye do well, and suffer for it, ye take it patiently, this is acceptable with God.

21 For even hereunto were ye called: because Christ also suffered for us, leaving us an example, that ye should follow his steps:"- (1 Peter 2:19-21)

Again I say if the Bible is clear on any subject, it is clear on the suffering of believers. However, it is not the kind of suffering that should be dreaded, but the kind that brings out the best of us because we are under His watchful care, and that He will not suffer us to be tempted above our ability to stand. When God knows that we have endured in our character building session long enough, He will deliver us and set us forth as examples for our generation. If you would notice, we are calling tests and trials "character builders" because that is what they are; they develop and stabilize us in our walk with the Lord. When we can remain steadfast under pressure, it is a good thing that we have found that secret place of the most high.

Considering taking on (or being like) the character of the Lord, we think of Him as never changing immutable, faithful. These are His character traits—marks of identification. Therefore, we want to be so molded that the same characteristics can be found in us. We would like to be known tomorrow for what we are today; that is, being dependable, righteous and faithful.

It is sad but true, there are so many Christians who have no real character; much of this lack is due to their desire to avoid anything that discomforts them. When we look back at Job, Satan was not questioning whether or not Job had character; he just wanted to test it to see how genuine it was. Job knew that he was not alone because he fell down and worshiped even after he had suffered great loss. Job gave us the key to spiritual success or survival-when things change we should turn our attention to One that will not change. Since the devil already hates us, we might as well give him a better reason to do so, by worshiping the Lord regardless of the circumstances.

Before I conclude, I want to say that there is a vast difference in the lifestyles of those who have been through the fire and those that came up the easy way. This principle holds true especially for those that are in the ministry. Assign an undeveloped minister to an established congregation, and if he or she does not already have character, the minister and the congregation will suffer greatly while he tries to develop character from that position. Many have been known to carry on without character and have made shipwreck of their lives and the lives of others. When opportunities are handed to someone on an already-forged silver platter, who has not been to Trouble U, and developed genuine character, failure is the proven results. This is one of the main reasons we have so many leaders with question marks behind their names. **We must understand that knowledge and talent are not substitutes for character.** Just because one can draw a crowd is no sign that he or she knows how to "acknowledge God in all his ways" or how to "go out and come in" before the people of God.

It is truly heart-breaking to see leaders whom we trust to help our souls, void of godly character. Guardedly, we had better not let them out of our sight with our daughters and sons because everyone that ministers the Word is not a man or woman of upright character. We can sum up many of today's clergy by saying that they have the talent of David but the integrity of Judas Iscariot. Let me add, I thank God that this picture may cover many but not all because God yet have men and women that are sold out, and who have purposed to hold out until Jesus calls them home.

It is clear to me why Jesus said that to follow Him one would have to deny himself, because self, too often, calls for things that are off limits to a Christian. To indulge would represent a detrimental effect to the character of a child of God. Any failure on our part cannot be blamed on the Lord; He will always do His part to keep us from falling or deliver us from all of our troubles. We will never walk alone no matter where our walk takes us. We can be sure that He is there every step of the way. The journey might take us through the flood, but He will be there; if through the fire, He is there; in sickness or death, we can count on His being there.

"Because he hath set his love upon me, therefore will I deliver him: I will set him on high, because he hath known my name.

15 He shall call upon me, and I will answer him: I will be with him in trouble; I will deliver him, and honour him."- (Ps 91:14-15)

We can say, according to the Word of God, that loving Him not only brings deliverance, but it also guarantees His presence with us in trouble and guarantees that we will be honored after it's all over. We all know that it would be good for Him to come along after trouble and minister to us, but He says He will be with us in trouble. Therefore, the next time you face one of your crisises please remind your problem that it has surrounded more than just you because you are not alone. Jesus is with you every step of the way. Just because Jesus is showing no signs or emotions, does not mean that He has abandoned you. It means that He is so confident that everything is going to be all right that there is not need to make any noise about it.

In the lions' den, the Lord did not remove the lions; He simply relaxed them so that they would not harm His servant Daniel. In the fiery furnace, the Lord did not extinguish the fire; He just tempered the heat by manifesting His presence with the young men in the fire.

When we are in our difficult situation, all we need is His presence manifested in us and victory is ours. He can just speak a word and we will be assured of victory. When Paul was caught in the storm, he told his traveling companions in so many words, *"I have heard from heaven."* Paul said an angel spoke with him in the night. What is needed in our time of trouble is the confidence that we are not alone and that the one that is with us is greater than any problem we will ever face.

GOD'S REPLY TO ANTICIPATED TROUBLE

1 Cor 10:13 There hath no temptation taken you but such as is common to man: but God is faithful, who will not suffer you to be tempted above that ye are able; but will with the temptation also make a way to escape, that ye may be able to bear it.

"Anticipate" = foreseeing and providing for before-hand, to know or expect in advance that something will happen or come into existence or be made manifest.

We can tell from the Word of God that trouble does not strike by surprise; the Lord has already fore-seen it coming and provided a way of escape for His trusting children.

What comes upon us might catch us by surprise but we can be sure that a way of escape has already been prepared by the Lord, we just need to trust Him and know that He has already checked out the thing before it comes upon us and He knows that we are able to withstand what He allows to come.

That is why we should not push the panic button because the Lord is in control, and He will not allow us to suffer that which we are unable to bear. Everything that comes upon us must first gain permission from Him. He only allows to come that which He knows we are able to endure. The Lord is committed to making us better. So He has to check every test and trial that comes upon His children, and He alone can determine what's best for the development of His dear ones.

Jesus taught His disciples that trouble was to be expected, in fact, He told them that they should rejoice when trouble comes upon them. He knew the reward of enduring trouble and riding out the storm, but it would only do so if met with the right attitude; this why He told them to rejoice and again I say, REJOICES.

Matt 5:11 Blessed are ye, when men shall revile you, and persecute you, and shall say all manner of evil against you falsely, for my sake.

12 Rejoice, and be exceeding glad: for great is your reward in heaven: for so persecuted they the prophets which were before you.

Luke 6:22 Blessed are ye, when men shall hate you, and when they shall separate you from their company, and shall reproach you, and cast out your name as evil, for the Son of man's sake.

23 Rejoice ye in that day, and leap for joy: for, behold, your reward is great in heaven: for in the like manner did their fathers unto the prophets.

If you notice, Jesus did not say if trouble should come because He knew that living right would bring all the trouble that His followers could hope for, they wouldn't have to go looking for it, it would come seeking after them for living right in this wrong world.

The followers of Jesus believed what He taught, we can see their examples in the Scriptures, and how they demonstrated that Jesus' teaching truly works for those who believe.

Acts 5:41 And they departed from the presence of the council, rejoicing that they were counted worthy to suffer shame for his name.

Jesus did not want His followers to feel that they were given a raw deal when trouble arose. He taught them to expect it and to rejoice upon its arrival. When one rejoices during his time of trouble, he receives divine strength to outlast his/her troubles. If we should give in by weeping, mourning, crying, sulking or complaining, our trouble will no doubt out last us. Rejoicing keeps us in a spiritual atmosphere and prevents the enemy from wearing us out. This is why we should rejoice.

Other advantages of trouble are often obscure to the human mind, but as we mature in the Lord, those seemingly difficult days are known to yields fruit of righteousness and godly character. That is why we must trust the Lord's wisdom in allowing trouble to come our way, He knows what's best for each of us, and He will not allow to come that which He knows would destroy us.

It is the devil who wants us to feel deserted, over matched and up against a wall that is too high for us to climb, he want us to be swallowed up with stress, fear, doubt and unbelief and end up quitting before we get started. Satan would do anything to keep us from knowing or understanding that the things that come upon us are going to work for our good. That is why the devil makes so much noise, he wants us to panic and throw in the towel. He want us to run like little scared chickens and forget that the greater one lives inside of us, but we refuse to allow these troubling circumstances to make us feel that God has left town without leaving His forwarding address. Testing times are as much a part of the Christian walk as material blessings are, the one satisfies while the other prepares us for advance service. Little do we realize that when we are asking the Lord to bless us and to use us, that we are in reality asking for an increase of trouble because God has always shown a willingness to have His vessels tested before He put them on display. Before David killed a giant, he first slew a lion and a bear; this was all behind the scene. After destroying the lion and bear, he was then ready to be brought to the forefront so that he could, before the eyes of God's trembling army, kill a giant.

God was so mighty in the destroying of the lion and the bear that David was fearless when time came to face the giant. The killing of the bear and the lion could be looked upon as a test run for meeting stronger opposition.

When we learn to trust the Lord, we rise from beginners faith to a higher level of faith, because we all start off with a measure of faith, and what we do with the measure we are given can be seen when we put it to work. If we feed our faith, it grows. We then, like David, be come successful when no one else is around and in the eyes of the multitude. God trained David on the backside of the desert, He allowed him to have test runs with trouble, and when the main event rolled around, he didn't have any trouble. He saw that the task was different but that his God was the same.

I believe with all of my heart that God would have us to understand that each trial, difficulty, hardship, opposition and testing is designed to move us up to take on the real challenge that comes our way. How well we do when no one is looking is the thing that increases our faith to deal with whatever comes regardless to who is looking.

Trouble is a training ground for patience. The more trouble we have, the more our patience will increase. We learn in the times of trouble that the Lord is not short when it comes to His promises. He will do exactly what He said He would do. All we have to do is to make sure that our anchor is in

Him and get ready to out last the next storm that life brings our way. *Because true patience is the ability to out last our troubles.* It is good for us to understand that the more trouble we have, the more our patience develops. Since that is true, it just might be that we need more trouble.

> *"And not only so, but we glory in tribulations also: knowing that tribulation worketh patience;"- Rom 5:3*

> *"And the Lord said, Simon, Simon, behold, Satan hath desired to have you, that he may sift you as wheat:*

> *32 But I have prayed for thee, that thy faith fail not: and when thou art converted, strengthen thy brethren."- (Luke 22:31-32)*

It was Jesus who told Peter that Satan desired to have him, and He did not promise Peter that He would stop the devil from attacking him; but He did tell Peter that He had prayed that his faith would not fail. Jesus knew that an attack from the wicked one would develop something in Peter that was missing; this is why Jesus told Peter that when he was converted he was to strengthen the brethren. Jesus was relying on Peter being better after his encounter with the devil. All that needed to happen was for Peter's faith to remain in tact. As long as he could put his trust in the Lord, he would overcome the enemy's attack.

We might try to conjecture why the Lord would allow the devil to attack His chief spokesman? We can see from the language that Satan wanted to sift him. It has been my observation that things are sifted to have the undesirable parts removed. Peter's case seems no different.There were some flaws in Peter's character that were not good for the kingdom the Lord was preparing him to operate in. And when Satan got finished sifting, the part that was left would be good enough to strengthen the brethren. Tried and tested people are good for the kingdom because they have had much of the undesirable shaken out of their lives. They know now how important it is to lean and depend on Jesus and not to trust in the arm of flesh.

"Forasmuch then as Christ hath suffered for us in the flesh, arm yourselves likewise with the same mind: for he that hath suffered in the flesh hath ceased from sin;

2 That he no longer should live the rest of his time in the flesh to the lusts of men, but to the will of God."- (1 Peter 4:1-2)

We can see from Peter's writings that the sifting of Satan only positioned him to speak words that are beneficial for the growth of the saints. He knew from his encounter that the rest of us could get ready by conditioning our minds for Satan's attacks. He helps us by informing us that the attacks of the devil work to reduce our fleshly sins and aids in the promotion of God's will.

Peter learned much from the attack of Satan upon his life, and just as Jesus said, Peter set out to strengthen the brethren. Let us consider more of Peter's words to the church:

"Beloved, think it not strange concerning the fiery trial which is to try you, as though some strange thing happened unto you:

13 But rejoice, inasmuch as ye are partakers of Christ's sufferings; that, when his glory shall be revealed, ye may be glad also with exceeding joy.

14 If ye be reproached for the name of Christ, happy are ye; for the spirit of glory and of God resteth upon you: on their part he is evil spoken of, but on your part he is glorified."- (1 Peter 4:12-14)

We can truly say that these are words from a man of much experience. He writes from what he knows and not just from what he heard someone say. If we give heed to what Peter is saying, we shall be better prepared when the devil launches his next attack on us—that we should not think it unusual when we are attacked because none of God's children are immune to trouble. When we take the attitude that we shouldn't have to go through the things that we suffer, we give assistance to the devil because he want us to feel that we are getting a raw deal from God and that we should turn aside from following

Him. If we listen to Peter, we would be miles ahead of Satan's game; we will know that rejoicing is much better than complaining.

Peter was the one that warned the church to watch out for the devil because he is on the prowl; he is looking for some victims to tear apart. Peter knew that the devil would have to seek out the particular ones to attack—those drunk with surfeiting, those not watching. If you are next, you can acknowledge that you have been forewarned to look out for the devil. Peter informs us that the enemy's attacks are universal. He also tells us that standing steadfast results in our being made stronger than we ever were before; he learned this from his encounters, and he freely passes it on to us so that we can out last the devil's testing.

> *"Be careful-watch out for attacks from Satan, your great enemy. He prowls around like a hungry, roaring lion, looking for some victim to tear apart.*
>
> *9 Stand firm when he attacks. Trust the Lord; and remember that other Christians all around the world are going through these sufferings too.*
>
> *10 After you have suffered a little while, our God, who is full of kindness through Christ, will give you his eternal glory. He personally will come and pick you up, and set you*

firmly in place, and make you stronger than ever."- (1 Peter 5:8-10) TLB

It is impossible to read the Bible without detecting that the people that were greatly used by God were often attacked by difficulties, trials and troubles. On that list you will find the Apostle Paul, a man greatly used by God but often attacked by Satan trying to prevent him from doing all the good that he could. We can tell from Paul's words that he was by no means intimidated by the devil's attacks, the more the enemy attacked Paul, the more he strove to help the saints.

"Are they ministers of Christ? (I speak as a fool) I am more; in labours more abundant, in stripes above measure, in prisons more frequent, in deaths oft.

24 Of the Jews five times received I forty stripes save one.

25 Thrice was I beaten with rods, once was I stoned, thrice I suffered shipwreck, a night and a day I have been in the deep; 26 In journeyings often, in perils of waters, in perils of robbers, in perils by mine own countrymen, in perils by the heathen, in perils in the city, in perils in the wilderness, in perils in the sea, in perils among false brethren;

27 In weariness and painfulness, in watchings often, in hunger and thirst, in fastings often, in cold and nakedness.

28 Beside those things that are without, that which cometh upon me daily, the care of all the churches."- (2 Cor 11:23-28)

I am sure that the Apostle Paul angered the devil over and over again because the more the devil fought him, the more he produced. Paul kept a good attitude toward what was happening, he was a man that seemed to expect trouble to come and when it did; he met it head on with boldness and courage.

"But we have this treasure in earthen vessels, that the excellency of the power may be of God, and not of us.

8 We are troubled on every side, yet not distressed; we are perplexed, but not in despair;

9 Persecuted, but not forsaken; cast down, but not destroyed;

10 Always bearing about in the body the dying of the Lord Jesus, that the life also of Jesus might be made manifest in our body.

11 For we which live are alway delivered unto death for Jesus' sake, that the life also of Jesus might be made manifest in our mortal flesh."- (2 Cor 4:7-11)

Paul understood that sufferings brought more of the likeness of Jesus into ones life, and that is what he wanted above all else, he was fascinated with the life of Jesus from start to finish.

"But what things were gain to me, those I counted loss for Christ.

8 Yea doubtless, and I count all things but loss for the excellency of the knowledge of Christ Jesus my Lord: for whom I have suffered the loss of all things, and do count them but dung, that I may win Christ,

9 And be found in him, not having mine own righteousness, which is of the law, but that which is through the faith of Christ, the righteousness which is of God by faith:

10 That I may know him, and the power of his resurrection, and the fellowship of his sufferings, being made conformable unto his death;

11 If by any means I might attain unto the resurrection of the dead.

12 Not as though I had already attained, either were already perfect: but I follow after, if that I may apprehend that for which also I am apprehended of Christ Jesus." - (Phil 3:7-12)

It was Paul's insight concerning suffering that made him a great success in his times of afflictions. Not once does he sound like trouble is getting the best of him, but to the contrary, he sounds as if trouble is advancing him toward the goal that has been set by the Lord Jesus Christ. He proclaimed, ".......forgetting those things which are behind, reaching forth unto those things which are before, I press toward the mark for the prize of the high calling of God in Christ Jesus". Through the revelation of the Spirit of God, the Apostle Paul makes it clear that the sufferings of this present world are a drop in the bucket compared to the glory that followers receive. In other words, the Apostle feels that the benefits of sufferings are grander than our short lived earthly afflictions, for that reason we shouldn't ever talk about suffering, we should talk about the glory that suffering brings.

Rom 8:18 For I reckon that the sufferings of this present time are not worthy to be compared with the glory which shall be revealed in us. KJV

Only the one sold out can see through the rough places in life, and know that nothing Satan brings can ever offset what the Lord is doing in the lives of

151

His children. Somewhere in Paul's life, he learned that the Lord doesn't have to take away one's afflictions, He can supply enough grace to enable one to continue without fainting and keep right on giving God the praises that He so rightly deserve.

"For though I would desire to glory, I shall not be a fool; for I will say the truth: but now I forbear, lest any man should think of me above that which he seeth me to be, or that he heareth of me.

7 And lest I should be exalted above measure through the abundance of the revelations, there was given to me a thorn in the flesh, the messenger of Satan to buffet me, lest I should be exalted above measure.

8 For this thing I besought the Lord thrice, that it might depart from me.

9 And he said unto me, My grace is sufficient for thee: for my strength is made perfect in weakness. Most gladly therefore will I rather glory in my infirmities, that the power of Christ may rest upon me.

10 Therefore I take pleasure in infirmities, in reproaches, in necessities, in persecutions, in distresses for Christ's sake: for when I am weak, then am I strong. - (2 Cor 12:6-10)

When God told Paul that His grace was sufficient, that was all Paul needed to activate his rejoicing modem. He knew once you get God's word on a matter, you can shift focus to something else because the Lord will do His part to bring to past that which is best for the lives of His children. If suffering is good for us, we can be sure that our time of suffering will come our way but with the suffering comes the watchful eyes of God to safeguard our lives to make sure that sufficient grace is applied in due time.

Paul had seen saints suffer at his hand before becoming a follower of the Lord Jesus. He saw Stephen stoned, he could not help but see the expression on Stephen's face as he drew his last breath, calling on the name of the Lord Jesus. This wonderful sight no doubt marked Paul for eternity. Paul was told the day he was baptized that he would suffer many things for the name of Christ, he armed himself for whatever the devil chose to bring and he finished his course with flying colors of success.

"For I am now ready to be offered, and the time of my departure is at hand.

7 I have fought a good fight, I have finished my course, I have kept the faith:

8 Henceforth there is laid up for me a crown of righteousness, which the Lord, the righteous judge, shall give me at that day: and not to me only, but unto all them also that love his appearing."- (2 Tim 4:6-8)

What consoling words spoken by one that had a lifetime of troubles, but wouldn't allow his afflictions to make him bitter, they instead made him better; they made him ready for his mansion prepared by his Lord.

This text has been used in countless numbers of home goings and funerals. In many cases the person being eulogized may not have fought at all, and if they did, it was not on the level that the Apostle fought. The Apostle was not just talking; he was expressing at death, the same confidence he had demonstrated during his entire saved life. He lived ready to face whatever life brought and died ready for whatever eternal life had to offer.

In my mind, the way the Apostle Paul lived, is by far the best way to live because living right prepares the way for dying right. This substantiates the truth that Paul's closing words are not befitting for every dead person. They are only appropriate for those who have truly fought sin on every hand until the last breath departs the body.

To avoid esteeming this testimony lightly—of rejoicing when trial, affliction and trouble comes upon us—all that person has to do is go to the Word of God and see the examples left on record. They would see that Jesus taught it and the disciples caught it and passed it on to us, now we need to practice it and pass it on to the generation following us.

"And they departed from the presence of the council, rejoicing that they were counted

worthy to suffer shame for his name."
- (Acts 5:41)

To make sense of suffering, the Lord promised those that suffered with Him the privilege of reigning with Him. This is why Paul could say that the suffering of this present life shouldn't even be compared to the glory that results from suffering. Now the enemy would like for us to feel that what we are feeling during our period of suffering is more severe than the benefits are rewarding. But we know better because we have the Lord's word on the matter.

"And not only so, but we glory in tribulations also: knowing that tribulation worketh patience;"- (Rom 5:3)

One hope of glory we have in suffering is we have the Lord's word that He will be in there with us, and secondly, the reward we gain will make the toil of the road seem as nothing. God is not like an over zealous parent, that shouts to a child "give me that knife," but has nothing to replace what was taken from the child. When the Lord allows something to be taken from us, He replaces it with something so much better, that we would hardly miss what was taken.

"My brethren, count it all joy when ye fall into divers temptations;

3 Knowing this, that the trying of your faith worketh patience."- (James 1:2-3)

Furthermore, we are so surrounded by examples of sufferings in the Word of God that the moment we open our mouths to complain, the word points to someone that suffered to a degree that it would make our problems seem like child's play.

"Take, my brethren, the prophets, who have spoken in the name of the Lord, for an example of suffering affliction, and of patience.

11 Behold, we count them happy which endure. Ye have heard of the patience of Job, and have seen the end of the Lord; that the Lord is very pitiful, and of tender mercy."- (James 5:10-11)

Godly examples are good for us who are trying to do what is best for the kingdom, and what brings glory to the name of the Lord. Paul had forever imprinted in his mind the behavior of the saints that he had imprisoned and the stoning of Stephen to set the stage for his future in Christ. We can tell from his writings and his lifestyle he was a good student of the Holy Ghost. I am sure that he had to be shocked by the peaceful way in which the saints endured grief and sufferings inflicted on them by Saul's compatriots while he held their coats.

"But he, being full of the Holy Ghost, looked up steadfastly into heaven, and saw the glory of God, and Jesus standing on the right hand of God,

56 And said, Behold, I see the heavens opened, and the Son of man standing on the right hand of God.

57 Then they cried out with a loud voice, and stopped their ears, and ran upon him with one accord,

58 And cast him out of the city, and stoned him: and the witnesses laid down their clothes at a young man's feet, whose name was Saul.

59 And they stoned Stephen, calling upon God, and saying, Lord Jesus, receive my spirit.

60 And he kneeled down, and cried with a loud voice, Lord, lay not this sin to their charge. And when he had said this, he fell asleep."- (Acts 7:55-60)

In verse 58, we are told that the men laid their clothes at the feet of Saul, so he was there when Stephen was stoned even if he didn't take part in the stoning, he saw what was done and he saw how Stephen left this world calling on the name of Jesus

and asking forgiveness for those that were putting him to death.

I feel reasonable sure that the spectacle of Stephen's death followed Paul to his grave, he saw a genuine saint die without screaming, kicking and pleading, but rather praising and praying. From this lesson; Paul learned that the best way to answer a problem is by offering praise. I'm confident that this memory influenced Paul and Silas to pray and sing and praise at midnight. Stephen's beautiful home going provided them with the answer to this problem. It is impossible to complain and praise at the same time. Complaining helps the devil stay in business, but praising prepares a throne for the Lord to be seated in our midst.

If we allow what the devil does to us to shut our mouth, we are sure to die in our prison, but if we open our mouth and offer praise to the Lord, He is sure to send His angel to shake our bars and set us free. We should not allow our circumstances to dictate when or if we can offer praise to the Lord, we should do so out of obedience and thanksgiving. When we do, we can be sure that we are attracting the Lord's attention and presence; He is known to show up where praises are known to go up. It is impossible for one to lift up Jesus and remain down because the higher we lift Him, the higher He will take the lifters. If you are at your lowest point, you need to immediately begin to lift up the name of Jesus in praise because your next move is up since you are already at the bottom. Whenever we are tempted to fret or complain, we need only to look at what the word says about afflictions and what they do and how long they last.

"For all things are for your sakes, that the abundant grace might through the thanksgiving of many redound to the glory of God.

16 For which cause we faint not; but though our outward man perish, yet the inward man is renewed day by day.

17 For our light affliction, which is but for a moment, worketh for us a far more exceeding and eternal weight of glory;

18 While we look not at the things which are seen, but at the things which are not seen: for the things which are seen are temporal; but the things which are not seen are eternal."- *(2 Cor 4:15-18)*

If a man that had suffered as many things as the Apostle Paul had could call afflictions light, we should be even the more able to agree with him, but he tells us how to deal with afflictions when they come upon us, we are to focus on the eternal aspect of what is produced by our afflictions, we must see them as temporary and not life lasting.

We should keep in mind that after ever testing comes triumph, if we want to excel, we must first be tried.

"Wherein ye greatly rejoice, though now for a season, if need be, ye are in heaviness through manifold temptations:

7 That the trial of your faith, being much more precious than of gold that perisheth, though it be tried with fire, might be found unto praise and honour and glory at the appearing of Jesus Christ:"- (1 Peter 1:6-7)

When we put our full confidence in the Word of God, we can determine the outcome before the battle is over because what God has said to one He says to all of His believing ones.

"Who shall separate us from the love of Christ? shall tribulation, or distress, or persecution, or famine, or nakedness, or peril, or sword?

36 As it is written, For thy sake we are killed all the day long; we are accounted as sheep for the slaughter.

37 Nay, in all these things we are more than conquerors through him that loved us.

38 For I am persuaded, that neither death, nor life, nor angels, nor principalities, nor powers, nor things present, nor things to come,

39 Nor height, nor depth, nor any other creature, shall be able to separate us from the love of God, which is in Christ Jesus our Lord."- (Rom 8:35-39)

The Lord doesn't conceal the fact that believers are to be tried. He, rather, informs us to that end. The reason that He can afford to make known that we are to be tried is because it is the only way that we can triumph and He causes us to always triumph in Him. We are conquerors with a plus sign. We are sure to be left standing when everything is over because we are in Him and there is no failure in God.

Again I say, that suffering is as much a part of the Christian walk as eating is a part of life, if we fail to eat we are sure to die, if we fail to suffer with Christ, we are sure to miss out on our crown.

"For unto you it is given in the behalf of Christ, not only to believe on him, but also to suffer for his sake;"- (Phil 1:29)

"But part of my work is to suffer for you; and I am glad, for I am helping to finish up the remainder of Christ's sufferings for his body, the Church."- (Col 1:24 TLB)

"So be truly glad! There is wonderful joy ahead, even though the going is rough for a while down here.

7 These trials are only to test your faith, to see whether or not it is strong and pure. It is being tested as fire tests gold and purifies it-and your faith is far more precious to God than mere gold; so if your faith remains strong after being tried in the test tube of fiery trials, it will bring you much praise and glory and honor on the day of his return."-(1 Peter 1:6 -7 TLB)

It is clear to me that trouble is the material that our crowns are made of, so we need to keep on believing even when all hope seems lost. We can be sure that the devil will, for sure, offer us an easier plan—a less painful way to spiritual success—but it's just like everything else that he has; it is strictly something to promote his agenda.

If we are spiritual or wise, we will follow the pattern set forth in the 11th chapter of Hebrews:

"Women received their dead raised to life again: and others were tortured, not accepting deliverance; that they might obtain a better resurrection:" (Heb 11:35)

Their pattern: the women in the above text adhered to their hope of glory, not accepting the so-called deliverance offered them. They were looking forward to experiencing the resurrection. If our desire is to obtain what the Lord has to offer, we had better turn down what Satan is offering.

It is heart warming to know that every test, trial, problem, affliction and attack from the devil is carefully weighed by the Lord. Holding on to this hope, our attitude toward afflictions of all kinds that come our way are viewed very differently.

The Lord knows that when we live godly we are going to be attacked by the enemy. So He makes sure that what the devil brings is in accordance only with what we are able to carry, and at no time are the Lord's children ever overloaded, nor are we allowed to suffer longer than He has prepared them to endure.

May Jesus Christ be Praise forever!

ABOUT THE AUTHOR

Bishop Clifton Jones is the senior pastor of the Jerusalem Temple Church in Philadelphia, Ms. for almost 40 years. He is the diocesan Bishop of the 10th Episcopal District of the Pentecostal Assemblies Of The World Inc.

Bishop Jones is an anointed preacher, inspired teacher and a prolific writer. His training includes a B.R.E from Aenon Bible College, the Columbus, Ohio. Masters of Ministry from The Bethany Seminary in Dothan, Ala, and a Doctorate of Divinity from Louisiana Baptist University in Shreveport, La.

Bishop Jones has carried the Word of God through the United States and into many foreign countries; he has also played a major role in the organizing of several churches within the district.

Bishop's Jones ministry has been effective both inside and outside, he has conducted many tent revivals over the years and open air meetings that drew many souls to the Lord, he is highly sought after for speaking engagements, he may be reach at the following addresses:

10120 Road 2613 or 414 Ivy street both in Philadelphia, Ms. 39350 e-mail-cliftonbcj@aol.com
   Phone: 601-656-3173-601-259-2412-601-416-2632-601-656-5339 (fax-601-656-5335)

OTHER BOOKS BY
BISHOP CLIFTON JONES

THESE BOOKS MAY BE ORDERED IN THE FOLLOWING WAYS:

CHECK OUT OUR WEB SITE: jtchurch.com

JERUSALEM TEMPLE CHURCH
414 IVY STREET
PHILADELPHIA, MS 39350

601-656-5339-CHURCH PHONE
601-656-9459-SECT.
601-416-2632 CELL

E-MAIL: cliftonbcj@aol.com
FAX: 601-656-5335
Mayfrancesjones@aol.com

YOU MAY MAIL ORDER ANY OF OUR MATERIAL BY WRITING US AT

JERUSAMEM CHURCH 414 IVY STREET PHILADELPHIA, MS. 39350

PRAYER CLINIC MANUEL

FAITH CLINIC MANUEL

LORD HEAL ME FROM THE INSIDE

HOW TO KEEP THE DEVIL OUT OF YOUR BUSINESS

I THOUGHT IT WAS THE DEVIL BUT IT WAS ME TOO

FASTING AND PRAYER FOR CHANGE

IT'S ALL ABOUT LOVE

A LITTLE KINDLING FOR YOUR FIRE

YOU NEED TO GROW UP

TOUGH FAITH

SOBER ADVICE FOR LAST DAY LIVING

FALLING IN THE WRONG PLACES

DYING AT THE DOCTORS DOOR

MISTAKING IDENTITY

ARE YOUR INDICTING ME?

PRAYER CLINIC WORKBOOK

FAITH CLINIC WORKBOOK

RUT OR REVIVAL

UNDER ATTACK BUT EQUIPTED TO STAND

IS IT OLD FASHION OR SAFE SANCTIFICATION?

GOD'S MEDICINE FOR THE WHOLE FAMILY

HOW PREACHERS COMMITT SUCIDE

Printed in the United States
81839LV00001B/175-999